Young Writers at T

G000154382

Young Writers at Transition tracks a group of pupils through from the end of Year 6 into the first half of Year 7. The book analyses in detail the teaching and uses of writing at this important stage in their education, and uncovers some revealing findings concerning the experiences, perceptions and expectations of pupils, teachers and parents about writing.

The author links the findings to the broader issues of policy and our understanding about how writing is taught and used at transition. This timely book examines issues such as:

- Transition, continuity and progression, and how these can be managed to ensure standards do not suffer;
- The variety of teaching and uses of writing in Years 6 and 7;
- Secondary school teachers' views of writing, and what practice is most effective for them.

This interesting study of the uses of writing will be a valuable resource to teachers and educators in primary and secondary schools. The book will also be of interest to those studying to be teachers.

Daniel Tabor is a Head of English at an 11–16 comprehensive school.

Language and Literacy in Action Series
Series Editor: David Wray

Young Writers at Transition

Daniel Tabor

For David and Brenda,
with love and best wishes
from Daniel
May 2004

rf RoutledgeFalmer
Taylor & Francis Group

LONDON AND NEW YORK

First published 2004
by RoutledgeFalmer
11 New Fetter Lane, London EC4P 4EE

Simultaneously published in the USA and Canada
by RoutledgeFalmer
29 West 35th Street, New York, NY 10001

RoutledgeFalmer is an imprint of the Taylor & Francis Group

© 2004 Daniel Tabor

Typeset in Sabon by
Keystroke, Jacaranda Lodge, Wolverhampton
Printed and bound in Great Britain by
TJ International Ltd, Padstow, Cornwall

British Library Cataloguing in Publication Data
A catalogue record for this book is available from the British Library

Library of Congress Cataloging in Publication Data
Tabor, Daniel C.
    Young writers at transition/Daniel Tabor.
        p. cm. — (Language and literacy in action series)
Includes bibliographical references (p.) and index.
        1. English language—Composition and exercises—Study and
teaching (Elementary)—Great Britain—Case studies. 2. English
language—Composition and exercises—Study and teaching
(Secondary)—Great Britain—Case studies. I. Title. II. Series.
LB1576 .T213 2004
372.62′3—dc22
                                                                2003019135

ISBN 0–415–25178–8 (pbk)
ISBN 0–415–25177–X (hbk)

To Hazel

Contents

List of illustrations

Figures

x *List of illustrations*

Tables

Series editor's preface

David Wray, University of Warwick

There can be few areas of educational endeavour which have been more controversial than that of teaching literacy. Perhaps because, in an increasingly information-dense society, the ability to make sense of and to produce text is self-evidently crucial to success, even survival, literacy has assumed the major burden as a litmus test of 'educatedness'. With such a critical role in the process of becoming educated, it is inevitable that there will continue to be major debates about exactly what it means to be literate, and about how such a state might most effectively be brought about – that is, how literacy is taught. A proportion of the energy behind such debates has come from the diverse findings of research into processes and pedagogy. Yet much of the debate, especially in the popular media, has lacked a close reference to research findings and has focused instead on somewhat emotional reactions and prejudices.

Students of literacy and literacy education who want to move beyond the superficiality of mass media debates need access to reports and discussions of key research findings. There is plenty such material, yet it tends to suffer from two major problems. Firstly, it can be rather difficult to locate as it has tended to be published in a diverse range of academic journals, papers and monographs. Secondly, research reports are usually written for an academic audience and make great demands on practitioners and others who wish to understand the practical classroom implications of what the research reports.

It is to address both these problems, but especially the latter, that this series has been developed. The books in the series deal with aspects of the teaching of literacy and language in a variety of educational settings. The main feature of all the contributing volumes is to provide a research-grounded background for teaching action in literacy and language. The books either, therefore, provide a review of existing research and theory, or an account of original research, in an area, together with a clear résumé and/or set of suggestions as to how this background might influence the teaching of this area. The series acts therefore as a bridge between academic research books and practical teaching handbooks.

Young Writers at Transition

In this volume Daniel Tabor addresses an issue which has not been given the attention it deserves. The institution, in 1988, of a National Curriculum in England and Wales was, in part, intended to ameliorate problems about the continuity of pupils' learning experiences as they moved from primary to secondary school. Unfortunately, there remain problems with this continuity and a number of research studies have suggested that the experience of pupils as they enter the first year of the secondary school rarely actively builds upon that of their primary years. Schools and teachers in both phases of schooling do not talk to each other enough and pupils' experience tends to be one of discontinuity rather than smooth transition. Daniel Tabor explores the complex reasons why this is so, and why these problems have persisted (to varying degrees) in spite of the National Literacy Strategy.

Daniel Tabor approaches the issue of primary–secondary transition by focusing on the teaching and learning of writing. Given the salience of this activity in both phases of schooling, one might expect that the continuity of experience would be a great deal better for pupils than in many other areas. Daniel Tabor's research, however, suggests that this is not the case. As well as poor communication between schools and teachers about pupils' achievements in writing, there are other factors which affect curriculum continuity. They include different teaching and learning styles, curriculum specialisms, and different expectations of the writing skills needed to be a successful learner in Years 6 and 7.

In the book, Daniel Tabor explores the issues of continuity and transition in writing, both as a researcher and as a teacher. He questions the way progression is conceptualised in the National Curriculum, and the implications this has for children's writing at the primary–secondary divide. Perhaps even more importantly, he goes on to make a great many suggestions as to how both primary and secondary teachers might act to improve the situation. Teachers from both phases of schooling, and from a range of subject bases, will find this a stimulating and useful book. It will challenge their existing practice and assist them in making positive steps towards improving it.

Acknowledgements

I wish to acknowledge the support of the teachers, pupils and parents who helped me with patience and humour while I conducted my research. Without their co-operation and generosity I would not have been able to carry out the fieldwork.

This book is based on the research I conducted for my PhD at the University of Warwick. I am very grateful to Professor Jim Campbell and Professor David Wray for their inspiring supervision and support. I have learned a great deal from both supervisors, and they provided me with an excellent research training. I am also grateful to Dr Angela Packwood, who supervised me at the early stages of this project. Thanks are also due to the Institute of Education, University of Warwick, for awarding me a scholarship.

I am grateful to the following colleagues at school for acting as critical readers of different chapters: Sarah Bowler, Liz Bray, Lynda Jones, Joan Mackness and Christine Vincent. I am also grateful to Phyllis and Fiona for moral support. I am indebted to Dr P. Manford (BASS) for information and advice about the 'Moving On Up' initiative, described in Chapter 8. The feedback I received from colleagues was very helpful when I redrafted the chapters, though the final version of the book, and any mistakes it may contain, are my responsibility. I am grateful to Alan Tero and Diana Legg for help with the figures in Chapter 5. My biggest debt is to Hazel Johnson, whose support, encouragement and advice enabled me to complete this book.

Acknowledgements

Abbreviations

ADT	Art and Design Technology
APU	Assessment Policy Unit
BASS	Birmingham Advisory and Support Service
CATs	Cognitive Aptitude Tests
DES	Department of Education and Science
DfE	Department for Education
DfEE	Department for Education and Employment
DfES	Department for Education and Skills
ERA	Education Reform Act
HMCI	Her Majesty's Chief Inspector
HMI	Her Majesty's Inspectorate
HMSO	Her Majesty's Stationery Office
ICT	Information and Communication Technology
JPS	Jeremy Priestley School
LEA	Local Education Authority
NAAE	National Association of Advisors in English
NAPE	National Association for Primary Education
NATE	National Association for Teachers of English
NIAS	Northamptonshire Inspection and Advisory Service
NFER	National Foundation for Educational Research
NLS	National Literacy Strategy
NNS	National Numeracy Strategy
OFSTED	Office for Standards in Education
ORACLE	Observation Research and Classroom Learning Evaluation
PSVE	Personal, Social and Vocation Education
QCA	Qualifications and Curriculum Authority
SCAA	Schools' Curriculum and Assessment Authority
SCDC	Schools' Curriculum Development Committee
SEAC	School Examinations and Assessment Council
SENCO	Special Educational Needs Co-ordinator

SOED	Scottish Office Education Department
TES	Times Educational Supplement
WO	Welsh Office

1 Beginning at the beginning

'Begin at the beginning,' the King said gravely, 'and go on till you come to the end: then stop.'

Alice's Adventures in Wonderland, Chapter 12.

What this book is about

The King of Hearts had clearly grasped some of the features of the National Literacy Strategy, at least where the teaching of narrative was concerned. I shall attempt to follow his advice, because I am about to tell a story, or a series of interlocking stories. This book is about the teaching of writing in Years 6 and 7, and the perceptions and experiences of pupils, teachers and parents about the nature of writing. I am writing for fellow teachers and literacy managers, with the intention of identifying key issues and suggesting practical ways of improving curriculum continuity in the teaching and uses of writing at primary–secondary transition.

As an English teacher and Head of Department I have worked closely with primary colleagues over many years, and for ten years members of my department and primary colleagues jointly planned projects involving primary and secondary pupils working together (Tabor 1991). I became very interested in the differences in teaching and learning styles between primary and secondary schools and the impact these differences had on pupils' learning as they moved to the secondary school.

This book describes in detail the writing experiences of four pupils as they moved from Year 6 to Year 7. It includes classroom observation; interviews with pupils, teachers and parents; and a survey carried out at two secondary schools. It is placed within a broader context of national reports and the findings of research on transition, continuity and progression between primary and secondary schools; the teaching and uses of writing; the pressure from the government on teachers to raise standards; and the impact of the National Literacy Strategy. The National Literacy Strategy (NLS) in primary schools initially concentrated on reading; the more recent shift to develop the teaching of fiction and non-fiction writing has made the focus on writing in this book particularly timely. However, I suggest that continuity and progression between primary and secondary schools continue to be problematic in spite of the introduction of the NLS, and I discuss the possible reasons for this state of affairs.

Literacy and standards

Invariably any discussion of literacy (and numeracy) cannot be separated from the government's repeated desire to raise standards. League tables, test results from Key Stages 1–3, and public examination results at the end of Key Stage 4 and 5 are used as evidence to identify where improvements in standards have occurred, and where further improvements need to be made. For teachers in secondary schools the rise (or improvement) in Key Stage 2 results has led to an irresistible pressure on Key Stage 3 results.

The culture of testing has come to preoccupy teachers, governors and parents to an extent that could not have been imagined five years ago. Gone are the days when the English Inspector in the county in which I teach issued a rallying cry to all Heads of English to boycott the Key Stage 3 national tests on the grounds that they were educationally harmful. It is difficult to believe that such a rebellion ever happened, and like the subjugated animals at the end of *Animal Farm* we now feel things have always been the same, at least where tests are concerned. Whatever our reservations about the English tests, we obediently prepare students for them, anxiously scrutinise the results, and discuss them with our senior managers.

Recent research suggests that the test results at Key Stages 2 and 3 are completely invalid as a reliable form of assessment (Wiliam 2001), though this view is not shared by the DfES. English Inspectors no longer have the scope to be independent, but act as channels for government policy, and the informal networks within an LEA and between schools have largely withered away. The success of the literacy and numeracy initiatives cannot be separated from the predicted improvement in test results at both Key Stages 2 and 3, and the government is unlikely to accept that these tests are conceptually flawed. Good test results may reflect good teaching (or at least good teaching to the tests) but the question that needs to be asked is whether the importance given to testing in its current form is the right priority where the education of our young people is concerned.

As a consequence of the improvement in Key Stage 2 test results, secondary teachers of English and Mathematics have been overwhelmed since the summer of 2001 with training sessions, glossy folders, and government directives to enable schools to improve literacy and numeracy across the curriculum, and hence raise standards (as measured through Key Stage 3 tests). LEAs, and primary and secondary schools, have had to set annual targets for national test results, linked to national targets. Within a period of three–five years the expectation is that the literacy and numeracy initiatives will become embedded in all aspects of teaching and learning in primary and secondary schools, and will contribute to a permanent improvement in standards. Recent changes in government policy, such as the decision to drop the primary targets (at Key Stage 2) for 2004, and the acknowledgement that tests for 7-year-olds need to be changed, suggest a more flexible approach (TES 2003). Whatever alterations may be made in the short term, the Secretary of State for Education has also made it clear that national tests and league tables are here to stay (e.g. Devo 2003: 24–5).

Building on pupils' previous achievements

One element or thread in this drive to raise standards is the repeated statement that the secondary schools need to build on the successes of primary schools, particularly at Key Stage 2. There is an expectation that if teachers do their job properly, there will be a year-on-year rise in national test results at both Key Stage 2 and Key Stage 3. It is in this context that secondary schools are exhorted to do more in terms of finding out what pupils have studied and achieved in Year 6, and using information from the primary schools to make the Year 7 curriculum more challenging. These strategies, it is argued, will motivate all students more effectively at the beginning of their careers as secondary school students, and hence contribute to the raising of standards at Key Stage 3. At face value this seems a reasonable expectation, but the reality of doing this is far more complex than the official pronouncements acknowledge.

Why is it that links between primary and secondary schools have been a relatively low priority for most secondary schools (a fact which predates the introduction of the National Curriculum)? The bottom line for most teachers, particularly of pupils in Year 6 and Year 7 is that, given all the other pressures they have to juggle with, cross-phase links are relatively unimportant, particularly if time is not made available to develop such links. For example, in Year 6 considerable time and effort are spent in preparing students for the Key Stage 2 tests, and teachers are also occupied with making teacher assessments and writing detailed end of year reports. At the beginning of Year 7 most subject teachers are concerned to induct the new students into 'their' ways of teaching and learning in English, geography, science, etc., and students are expected to learn the 'ground rules' (Sheeran and Barnes 1991) for these discrete subjects. Given that the new students will have come from many different primary or junior schools, the priority for the subject teacher in Year 7 is often to give the new student 'the basics' to ensure that everyone in the class starts the Key Stage 3 curriculum with (roughly) the same knowledge base.

Using writing as the focus for my argument, I will suggest that the relative lack of cross-phase and cross-curricular communication affects teaching and learning as pupils move from Year 6 to Year 7. With respect to writing, it might be argued that the Key Stage 3 Literacy Strategy is addressing these issues, and bringing teaching and learning styles at Key Stages 2 and 3 closer together. I will argue that the realities of teaching the secondary school curriculum make cross-phase and cross-curricular communication more difficult than the training manuals and official exhortations acknowledge. This is because the main pressure on secondary schools, particularly in the core curriculum subjects, is to deliver good examination results at the end of Key Stage 3, and to provide the foundations for the GCSE examinations at Key Stage 4. This is in spite of the good literacy practices which are emerging in secondary schools. Throughout the book I focus on what teachers can do to improve the teaching and learning of writing, including suggestions for the way forward.

Transition, continuity and progression

The notions of transition, continuity and progression have been discussed widely in official documents and the research literature. From the official perspective, adequate information and appropriate structures exist to support better curriculum continuity between primary and secondary schools. All that is required is for schools to do more, and to do it better. The research literature, on the other hand, shows that curriculum continuity and progression at transition continue to be problematic for pupils, teachers and parents. The reasons for this are complex and deep-seated, in spite of the introduction of the National Literacy and Numeracy Strategies. Furthermore, the issues of continuity and progression in the curriculum are often separated from the pastoral support new pupils usually receive when they move to the secondary school. The implications of this for the transformation of the primary school pupil into the successful secondary school student are considerable, given the different styles of induction programmes in secondary schools (Hargreaves and Galton 2002: 28–53).

There is much discussion (though not a lot of disagreement) about the extent of the Year 7 'dip', the evidence for this dip, and why it is significant for some Year 7 students. However, concern about the Year 7 dip also reveals broader issues about the lack of continuity and progression between primary and secondary schools. Secondary teachers may be a little cynical about the Year 7 dip, particularly since there is research evidence of a Year 8 'dip', and indeed there may be dips in pupils' achievements at the beginning of successive years of secondary education. There is also research evidence that suggests a dip in pupils' achievements occurs after the Key Stage 1 tests (Minnis *et al.* 1998). The Year 7 dip has attracted considerable attention for over 30 years, and it was one of the reasons for introducing the National Literacy and Numeracy Strategies at Key Stages 2 and 3. One could argue that the dip will occur anyhow, and that the majority of new pupils will make up the ground lost at the beginning of Year 7. However, a small number of pupils never catch up, and are (in effect) lost to the system (Galton *et al.* 1999a; Pollit 1999).

Why writing?

Historically the teaching of reading has received much more attention in terms of official guidance and reports, and in the research literature, than the teaching of writing. The reasons for this are not clear, but the teaching of writing has been seen by many educators as more difficult than the teaching of reading. Though the NLS in primary schools initially focused on the teaching of reading, almost at the expense of writing, this imbalance has been redressed, and both primary and secondary schools have been issued with guidance on the teaching of writing, the importance of grammar for writing, and the approaches that should be used in primary and secondary classrooms.

There are several models that have been influential in the development of theories about writing, and have contributed to recent government policy documents. The issues raised by these models of writing are important; not only do they affect the ways we teach and assess writing in English, but writing is used as a means of assessment in most subjects. How progression in writing has been conceptualised in policy documents and reports, and how this 'official' notion of progression is both similar to and different from the ways teachers and pupils conceptualise the notion of good writing, are significant for the raising of standards. The tension between policy and practice in the assessment of progression also has implications for the development of curriculum continuity between primary and secondary schools.

The discussion of writing has to take into account the gendered nature of boys' and girls' achievements. Girls continue to outperform boys in the national tests at Key Stage 2 and Key Stage 3, and more specifically, girls tend to be 'better' at writing than boys. Much research has been done on gender and literacy (e.g. Millard 1997), and the issue has been investigated by OFSTED (e.g. OFSTED 1993). The main focus of this book is not about gender differences in progression, but where appropriate I refer to boys' and girls' experiences of writing.

The study

This book is based on a study of the experiences of teachers and pupils across several subject areas in three schools. I tracked four pupils from the last term of Year 6 through to the middle of Year 7, observed the types of writing they produced in their lessons, and interviewed them about their perceptions and experiences of writing. I also tried to place the pupils in their family context by interviewing their parents or carers about the types of writing that took place at home. I interviewed a range of teachers about the teaching of writing, including those teaching the four pupils. In addition I conducted a survey in two secondary schools about teachers' attitudes and approaches to the teaching of writing in Year 7.

My research was conducted in Billesley, a town of approximately 23,000 inhabitants in the Midlands. It was originally a market town, which has expanded over the last 40 years with the influx of people mainly from Birmingham. There is a range of light industries, and low unemployment. The town contains two 11–16 comprehensive schools and a tertiary college. All the places, schools, adults and children referred to in this book have been given pseudonyms.

The book is thus based on a detailed local study, a 'thick description' (Geertz 1973). I relate it to other research findings, and identify the most important aspects of my findings which should be of interest to a reflective practitioner in the classroom, or a teacher with management responsibilities for whole-school literacy. The study was conducted between 1997 and 1998; however in 2002 I re-interviewed most of the teachers involved in the original study, to take account of changes which had taken place since the introduction of the National Literacy Strategy.

Some of the problems which I identified in 1998 in the teaching and uses of writing at primary–secondary transition appeared to persist (with modifications) four years later, and I consider the possible reasons for this.

Outline of book structure

In Chapter 2 I discuss the key issues about curriculum continuity and progression at transition. I contrast official pronouncements with the most important research findings. I also analyse the ways progression has been conceptualised in different models of writing, and the implications of this for the assessment of progression at transition. In Chapter 3 I discuss the types of writing that the pupils did in Years 6 and 7, and in Chapter 4 I consider the different approaches to the teaching and uses of writing that I observed in primary and secondary classrooms. Secondary school teachers' views of writing in 1998 and 2002 are analysed in Chapters 5 and 6 respectively. In Chapter 7 I analyse the differences and similarities between home writing and school writing, and suggest why these differences are significant for transition to the secondary school. In the final chapter I draw the different threads of the book together, and consider the implications of my book for policy and practice. I conclude Chapters 2 through to 8 with suggestions for the practising teacher.

There are many references to the world of Lewis Carroll in this book. His ability to describe surreal, absurd or nightmarish situations, and to explain them with apparently impeccable logic, seemed unexpectedly familiar. When considering the twists and turns of government policy in the context of my research, Carroll's humour has helped me to keep my sanity and sense of detachment.

The problematic nature of the relationship between policy and practice in the National Curriculum is one of the threads that runs through this book. I hope that colleagues with a reflective approach to the teaching of literacy, or those involved in managing the literacy agenda in schools, will find the issues raised in this book helpful in promoting the teaching and uses of writing. In one respect, I will not be following the King of Hearts' advice. Though this book has an end, the story I am telling does not stop at the last page. For each reader, I hope that reflection on the issues raised here about teaching and learning will continue long after the book has been closed.

2 Analysing the issues
Transition, continuity and progression

Then she began looking about, and noticed that what could be seen from the old room was quite common and uninteresting, but all the rest was as different as possible.

Through the Looking Glass, Chapter 1.

Introduction

When Alice climbed through the looking glass, she found that although the new room was similar in some respects to the old one, it was also far more interesting and exciting. One would like to think that this is a suitable metaphor for what happens when a pupil leaves the primary school and starts at the 'big' school. There may be similarities with what has gone before, but it should also be an adventure, a challenge, and a source of new experiences. This may be the case for some pupils, but the complexities of transition to the secondary school continue to concern teachers, pupils, researchers and policy makers.

The first part of this chapter discusses these complexities, and analyses the concepts of continuity, progression and transition at the primary–secondary interface. In the second part of the chapter I consider how progression has been conceptualised in different theories of writing; how the official notions of progression differ from the views of teachers and pupils; and the implications of this for pupils' progression at transition. In the third section of the chapter I analyse the research evidence about writing at transition, focusing on the expectations and experiences of teachers and pupils. The main argument of the chapter is that continuity and progression between primary and secondary schools have become more problematic since the introduction of the National Curriculum. I attempt to provide ways of thinking about these issues, both at theoretical and practical levels, and I consider some of the implications for practising teachers and their pupils at the end of this chapter.

As a working definition 'curriculum continuity' will be used in this book to describe the ways teachers plan and deliver the curriculum within and between years, while 'progression' will refer to the achievements of pupils as they move through the educational system. However, continuity can also refer to continuities in pupils' experiences as they move from one year to another, or move from primary or middle school to secondary school. This sense of continuity implies a 'building on' from what pupils achieved in the previous year or phase of education. Continuity and progression cannot therefore be considered in isolation from each other, and will often be discussed together in this book. I also discuss the concept of progression in more detail later in this chapter.

Underlying much research, and many official pronouncements, are assumptions (often implicit) about the nature of curriculum continuity, and how progression and pupils' achievements should be measured. The problematic nature of continuity between primary and secondary schools, and the implications this has for progression and raising standards, are part of a broader debate about the effect of the National Curriculum on teaching and learning (e.g. Campbell 1996). The main differences between the official rhetoric on curriculum continuity, progression and transition on the one hand, and the research findings on the other, are summarised in Table 2.1. The table highlights the underlying tension between the government's view that there are enough data at the end of Year 6 about pupils' attainments, combined with appropriate bridging initiatives, to promote successful curriculum continuity between Key Stages 2 and 3; and the research evidence which shows that establishing curriculum continuity between the phases is still complex and problematic. If you are a practising teacher, Literacy Manager or Consultant, or a PGCE student who has visited primary and secondary schools recently, you may wish to critique this table. Do you agree with the contrast I have drawn between the two perspectives? If not, how would you alter this table?

The historical context

Taking a historical perspective on curriculum continuity, progression and transition will enable us to see what has changed since the introduction of the National Curriculum; what underlying problems remain the same; and the implications for practice. Where curriculum continuity between primary and secondary schools was concerned, official reports (e.g. DES 1967, 1975, 1982), and research in the 20 years before the

Table 2.1 Official and research-based views of continuity and progression at the transition from primary to secondary school

Official documents	Research evidence
• There is evidence of a 'dip' in pupils' achievements in Year 7 that has persisted over the last 30 years, in spite of the introduction of the National Curriculum.	• There is evidence of a 'dip' in pupils' achievements in Year 7 that has persisted over the last 30 years, in spite of the introduction of the National Curriculum.
• Secondary schools need to build on the achievements of pupils at Key Stage 2 to promote better continuity and progression at the start of Year 7, thereby counteracting the 'dip'.	• A significant minority of pupils regresses during Year 7, and never catches up. They are, in effect, lost to the system.
• The information to support better planning of the Year 7 curriculum is available, in terms of Key Stage 2 test results and teacher assessments at the end of Year 6.	• Attempts to create working relationships between primary and secondary teachers about the curriculum have become more difficult over the last ten years, owing to increased workload.
• The Key Stage 2 test results are reliable.	• Secondary schools are not, on the whole, successful at communicating their expectations to new pupils before the start of Year 7. Pupils in Year 6, and their parents and teachers, are largely ignorant of what these expectations are, particularly in terms of the curriculum.
• It is assumed that the curriculum at Key Stage 2 and Key Stage 3 has remained relatively stable.	
• Schools need to do more to ensure that Key Stage 2 test results and other relevant information about new pupils are transmitted to the secondary school. This information should be circulated to the classroom teacher via the Head of Department, to facilitate curriculum planning in Year 7.	• Secondary school teachers distrust the Key Stage 2 test results and teacher assessments. If these data reach Year 7 teachers, they are unsure how to use them to inform curriculum planning.
• Clusters of primary and secondary schools need to make their own decisions about what types of additional information should be communicated to the secondary school, and when and how it should be transmitted.	• Most primary school teachers (especially in Year 6) think that their work is ignored or undervalued by the secondary schools.
	• Most secondary teachers feel that new pupils will not have been given an adequate grounding in their subject at Key Stage 2.

- In secondary schools, English, mathematics and science departments are recommended to analyse the Key Stage 2 test scores in detail before the start of Year 7, so that they can identify the strengths and weaknesses of new pupils.

- Teachers in Years 6 and 7 should moderate portfolios of pupils' work together, so that they can reach agreement about the nature of National Curriculum levels.

- Schools should use bridging units in English, mathematics and science to improve continuity and progression between Years 6 and 7 (DfES 2002).

- Summer schools will provide additional support for pupils who did not achieve Level 4 in the Key Stage 2 tests, and help them to make a more confident start at secondary school.

- Progress Units will help selected pupils to improve their literacy skills in Year 7, enabling them to access the Key Stage 3 curriculum more successfully.

- Many secondary teachers favour the 'fresh start' approach at the beginning of Year 7. Covering 'the basics' at the beginning of Year 7 is regarded by the teachers as a form of revision and consolidation. Good progress at Key Stages 3 and 4 can be built on these foundations.

- Key Stage 2 tests are 'high stake' tests for primary schools; Key Stage 3 tests are less important at secondary school than GCSE results.

- Pastoral liaison is usually well developed between primary/middle and secondary schools, and is successful in enabling pupils to adjust socially to their new school.

- It is difficult to use transition units when your secondary school receives pupils from dozens of primary schools, as in some inner-city schools (e.g. Templeton and Hood 2002).

introduction of the National Curriculum focused on the following issues:

- The difficulties of establishing continuity of curriculum content between different stages of education;
- The repetition of work in the secondary school that had already been attempted at primary school;
- What types of information should be transferred between different phases, and the ways it should be used;
- The approaches to pastoral liaison between schools that would enable children to settle in more easily in their new school.

The issues were particularly acute when considering primary–secondary transition because of the alleged differences in teaching and learning styles, and classroom organisation, between the two phases. The change from one teacher who delivered the curriculum through (largely) cross-curricular topics, to the secondary world of specialist teachers, presented (and still presents) pupils with a different teaching and learning environment.

Much research concentrated on the anxieties pupils experienced at transition, and the ways these anxieties could be reduced (e.g. Nisbet and Entwistle 1969; Youngman and Lunzer 1977; Jennings and Hargreaves 1981; Galton and Willcocks 1983; Youngman 1986). Research showed that most pupils made a successful adjustment to the new world of the secondary school by the end of their first term, through forming new friendships and adjusting to the different routines of the secondary school. In general, schools were successful in developing pastoral liaison with primary schools, and developing induction pro-grammes that made the process of 'settling in' easier for new pupils (e.g. Spencer 1988; Cumberland-Harper 1991). Pastoral liaison included the transfer of information about friendship groups, behaviour, high and low achievers, etc. Visits of new pupils to the secondary school were used to familiarise pupils with the new school before transition.

The main concern about transition and curriculum continuity was highlighted in the 1980s by the ORACLE project, which drew attention to the dip in achievement for the majority of pupils during their first year at the secondary school: 'For the great majority of pupils, levels of progress were reduced, and for many pupils actual losses were made' (Galton and Willcocks 1983: 93). Thus the ORACLE project confirmed the findings of earlier research, but studied in depth the possible causes of this dip, and explained it in terms of the differences in teaching and learning styles pupils encountered as they moved from primary to secondary school. These findings were confirmed by other research (e.g. Dodds and Lawrence 1984: 62) and raised the question of how curriculum continuity could be improved between the phases.

The National Curriculum and curriculum continuity

The introduction of the National Curriculum was intended to provide a seamless curriculum that would, with its programmes of study and assessment framework, provide continuity of the curriculum between the ages of 5–16 (e.g. DES 1989: 20). However, a number of official documents since the mid-1990s highlighted concerns that the National Curriculum had not greatly improved curriculum continuity between primary and secondary schools, in spite of the shared curriculum framework. Underlying these documents were assumptions about the validity of the Key Stage 2 tests (and a desire to refute criticisms of their validity), the value of the eight-level scale in describing pupils' achievements in the core subjects at the end of Year 6, and the usefulness of this information in helping teachers at secondary school plan the Year 7 curriculum. The main thrust of these documents was to place the onus on teachers and schools to make curriculum continuity and progression between primary and secondary schools more effective (e.g. SCAA 1996, 1997a, 1997b; QCA 1998a).

From the official perspective the main issues in promoting better curriculum planning and progression at the start of Year 7 were the efficient transmission and appropriate use of information from the primary school. In other words, if the administrative procedures were improved, Year 7 teachers would make appropriate use of the information provided, thus ensuring that pupils made better progress at the beginning of Key Stage 3.

The official approach was problematic because it was based on two main assumptions. First, that the Year 6 curriculum was assessed appropriately, and second, that the Year 6 curriculum was stable. Neither assumption was easily defensible, since the Key Stage 2 tests have been plagued by problems of reliability at least until 1996, when some standardisation was attempted (DfEE 1996), and the reliability of all the key stage tests was criticised by HM Chief Inspector (TES, 18 December 1998, p. 1). The introduction of the National Literacy and Numeracy Strategies since 1998 has also significantly altered the balance of curriculum provision at Key Stage 2. Furthermore, the implications for teachers' time and workload were hardly acknowledged, and restricting the focus to English, mathematics and science left unanswered the issues of continuity and progression in the non-core subjects. Moreover, research showed that the issues were far more complex than the official documents acknowledged, for example, the distrust most secondary teachers felt for Key Stage 2 assessments (e.g. Lance 1994; Jones 1995; Jarman 1997), and the widely held opinion that this information was irrelevant for curriculum planning at Key Stage 3 (e.g. Sutherland *et al.* 1996; Doyle and Herrington 1998).

Recent research studies have confirmed OFSTED findings that regression (or at least a hiatus) in pupils' progress as they move from primary to secondary school continues to be a problem (e.g. OFSTED 1998, 1999a). These research studies (e.g. Sutherland *et al.* 1996; Herrington and Doyle 1997; Suffolk LEA 1997; Marshall and Brindley 1998; Galton *et al.* 1999a; Pollit 1999; Hargreaves and Galton 2002) indicated a variety of contributory factors, such as:

- the inappropriate nature of the work pupils did at the start of Year 7;
- the extent to which secondary teachers failed to build on pupils' achievements at Key Stage 2;
- the different types of information transferred from primary to secondary schools;
- the ways this information was used (or more frequently not used) to support curriculum planning in Year 7;
- the lack of trust teachers in different phases had of each other's judgements;
- the distorting effect of preparing for the Key Stage 2 tests on the Year 6 curriculum; and
- the different models of English used at primary and secondary school, which made cross-phase communication between teachers more difficult.

We can see that since the introduction of the National Curriculum some of the concerns about curriculum continuity have changed. The content of the curriculum is not a source of major disagreement between primary and secondary teachers, whatever reservations they may have about the programmes of study, and the way creativity is squeezed out of the classroom, particularly in Year 6. The electronic transfer of information will eventually enable all secondary schools to create databases about new pupils containing their attainments at Key Stage 2. The introduction of the NLS and NNS and the Frameworks for English and mathematics at Key Stage 3 are intended to bring teaching and learning styles closer together across the primary–secondary divide. However, the issues for many secondary teachers are still whether they trust the primary school assessments (though for reasons that are different from the pre-ERA period); how this information is to be used at the start of Year 7 to avoid repetition of the curriculum; and the low priority in many schools for teachers to communicate cross-phase about teaching and learning.

Considering progression

Discussion of continuity and progression of pupils as they move from Key Stage 2 to Key Stage 3 assumes that there is a consensus as to what these concepts mean. The National Curriculum programmes of study provide a framework for continuity based on subject content and skills. The notion of progression which underpins this is

> based on some model of a pupil's increasing knowledge, skill and understanding within a particular learning (subject) domain. The underlying model is based on a notional 'typical pupil' and the broad stages of education that he or she passes through.
>
> (Nicholls and Gardner 1999: 28)

The National Curriculum assumes that progression can be defined in terms of the eight-level scale across key stages – implicitly a linear model of learning and progression. As Nicholls and Gardner commented 'it must be recognised that not all children progress at the same rate or along the same route' (Nicholls and Gardner 1999: 29). This is an issue within schools as well as between schools, though the difficulties become more acute when considering progression means across Key Stages 2 and 3.

What do we mean by progression? *The Concise Oxford Dictionary of Current English* defines progression as 'progressing; succession, series' and the definitions of progress include 'advance or development esp. to a better state' (Sykes 1982: 882). The definitions of development include 'gradual unfolding; growth; evolution…' (*ibid*.: 262). Progression and development are not the same, because the latter term carries with it the suggestion of growth, maturation and greater sophistication, while progression suggests a process of learning and improvement which results from direct teaching. Talk of progression is the result of a structured curriculum, with clearly signposted stages identifying what a 'typical' child should know or be able to do at each stage. It could be argued that this distinction between progression and development is somewhat arbitrary, as children undergo a complex process of maturation and personal development (intellectual, emotional, psychological) as they move through the school system. At the same time teachers would be failing if they could not show that pupils had made progress in their studies.

'Progress' (or progression – the terms are used here interchangeably) also needs to be distinguished from the idea of 'attainment'. Though progress and attainment are obviously connected in practice, they are conceptually distinct. 'Attainment refers to a pupil's performance at one single point in time, for example, performance in a national test in English at age 11' (Campbell 1996: 3). For example, the 'average' pupil might achieve or attain a Level 4 in the Key Stage 2 tests in English.

Progress is a more complex idea, because it refers to the change in attainment between two or more points in time, that is between

> a baseline measure of attainment and a later measure. We might take a pupil who at age 7 attained Level 2 in a national curriculum test in English, and who four years later, at age 11, attained Level 4 in a national curriculum test of English. Such a pupil could be said to have made progress equivalent to two national curriculum levels.
>
> (Campbell 1996: 3).

We should note that the use of 'measure' here suggests the idea of precision, of number, and these connotations are part of the official ethos of national curriculum tests, with its emphasis on statistics and published league tables.

The view of progress quoted above refers to pupils' changing attainments through time, but any model of the curriculum must be based on some assumptions about the most appropriate sequence of teaching and learning activities in a particular domain, and the order in which these activities should be presented to learners (Hughes 1995: 3). There are two related issues here: how do we conceptualise the nature of progression, and how do we measure it? A general discussion about the nature of progression raises questions such as: is progression mainly developmental (psychological, emotional, cognitive, etc.), how much is it to do with teaching and learning, how is it dependent on pupils' language competences, their socio-cultural background, or the social construction of the learning environment?

Progression in writing

In this book I am focusing on writing, so that we can gain a better understanding of what happens to progression and continuity at primary–secondary transition. It is therefore appropriate in this section to consider how progression in writing has been conceptualised, and to relate this discussion to the broader issue of transition. Why writing? It is not simply that writing is an important aspect of the English curriculum, nor that it has received particular attention recently in the National Literacy Strategy. Looking across the curriculum, writing is one of the main means of assessing pupils' knowledge, skills and understanding. In the wider society, writing is often used as a metaphor for the process of education, or even being educated (with the connotation of passing rigorous public examinations).

What does it mean to be good at writing? The National Curriculum for English (to take one example) provides a model based largely on linguistic and grammatical correctness, and this is reflected in the annual commentaries on the national end-of-key stage English tests. But this is only one approach to conceptualising what being good or 'better' at writing can mean. We all talk about progression because it is so much part of the official rhetoric, along with the discussion of targets and other performance indicators, and it is easy to accept the jargon, and not to question the underlying ideas. The analysis of progression in writing has been the subject of extensive debate, often framed in terms of how children learn to write, and how they develop as writers, though writing development and progression in writing are not identical.

Many writers, particularly in the 1970s and 1980s, have discussed writing development rather than progression (e.g. Britton *et al.* 1975; Beard 1984; Wilkinson 1986a). Different aspects of writing were used as indices of development in writing. For example, some studies concentrated on the linguistic features of children's writing (e.g. Harpin 1976; Perera 1984); the cognitive, affective and moral development in children's writing (Wilkinson *et al.* 1980); the development of planning (Burtis *et al.* 1983), spelling (e.g. Henderson 1981), or uses of vocabulary (e.g. Harpin 1976; Beard 1984); the changing structural organisation of children's stories or reports (e.g. Applebee 1978; Langer 1986). Researchers identified patterns as to how children performed different writing tasks, and related these to different developmental 'stages'. The notion of developmental stages in writing owed much (whether at an implicit or explicit level) to the developmental theories of Piaget (1926) and Chomsky (1965), where the child's language development was seen as being driven by an innate desire or need to make sense of the world. The most important models or theories of writing, and their influence on the conceptualisation of progression in the National Curriculum and the National Literacy Strategy, are analysed in Table 2.2.

Table 2.2 Conceptualising progression in writing

Theory or model of writing	Key points	Conceptualisation of progression in writing	Influence on policy	Other comments
Writing functions (Britton et al. 1975).	Model of writing continuum, based on idea of writing functions: expressive, transactional and poetic. Expressive writing: 'seed bed' out of which the other two functions could grow. Transactional writing: used to 'get things done', e.g. settle an argument. Poetic writing: identified with the production of literature.	No model of writing progression. Emphasis on writing development as a process of maturation, linked to the development of the child's thought processes.	Categories of writing functions and audience influenced the Bullock Report (DES 1975), and indirectly the development of the National Curriculum (NC).	Focus on writing products, not processes. Britton's writing continuum existed independently of the social world of the pupil and teacher. Britton's model did not explain how children could learn to write in different genres.
Writing development linked to the personal growth and maturity of the child (e.g. Wilkinson et al. 1983, Wilkinson 1986a, 1986b).	Creative writing as a means of furthering personal growth. Emphasis on the pupil using his/her imagination. Cognitive, affective, moral and stylistic models of language development were used to provide evidence of the personal growth of a 'typical' pupil (Wilkinson et al. 1980).	No account of progression in writing. The child's writing development unfolded 'naturally' as he/she matured.	No direct influence, though the writing of poetry, recounts, narrative, etc., may reflect the importance many teachers attach to creative writing.	No account of how children should be taught creative writing, or how to do it better.

Cognitive approaches: (Bereiter and Scardamalia 1987)	Focus on mental processes which accompany and produce writing. Importance of meta-cognition in helping writers to improve their writing. Difference between two writing processes: *knowledge telling* and *knowledge transforming*. Distinction between novice and expert writers.	Developmental view of writing, based on a view of adult writing competence. Transformation of a novice writer to an expert writer. Practical suggestions about the ways teachers can help pupils produce knowledge transforming writing, e.g. by use of teacher modelling.	No direct influence on the NC though the advocacy of teacher modelling and the importance of meta-cognition may have influenced the techniques for the teaching of writing in the National Literacy Strategy.	Raising pupils' awareness of writing processes may contribute to increased expertise in writing.
Socio-constructivist approaches (e.g. Street 1984, Garton and Pratt 1989, Barton 1994).	Different literacy practices are embedded in different social contexts. Many 'literacies', or at least a continuum of literacy practices. The social construction of writing in the classroom has an important effect in determining how children learn to write at school.	No model of writing progression.	Negligible. The NC and National Literacy Strategy emphasise the teaching of writing skills, irrespective of social context.	Emphasis on writing as a socially constructed practice, not as a cognitive skill to be taught and learned irrespective of social context. It may be useful to see both approaches as complementary, not mutually exclusive.

Table 2.2 continued

Theory or model of writing	Key points	Conceptualisation of progression in writing	Influence on policy	Other comments
The National Writing Project (NWP) (1985–1989).	At the time regarded as a model of good practice, not a theory of writing development. Emphasised the importance of writing for 'real' audiences and purposes. Editing and redrafting, conferencing, collaborative writing and publishing pupils' work were central to the NWP.	No theory of progression. Advocated a view of writing development that was recursive, i.e. 'pupils returning time and again to similar tasks, refining their ability in each case' (NWP 1989d: 92).	Emphasis on editing and redrafting, and writing for specific audiences and purposes, influenced the approach to writing in the NC.	Overwhelming emphasis on narrative. Only successful examples or case studies were reported. Not supported by explicit approaches to teaching pupils to write in a range of genres.
Linguistic approaches (e.g. Kress 1982, Perera 1984).	Analysis of linguistic differences in texts produced by children of different ages. These differences were linked to children's 'development' or relative 'maturity'.	No theory of progression in writing. Different phases in the acquisition of writing abilities were linked to a developmental continuum, especially in the early years. Theories acknowledge the difficulty of assigning chronological ages to these phases.	Increasing emphasis on linguistic analysis of pupils' writing in reports on end-of-key stage tests, and other official documents. Linguistic features of children's writing identified with NC levels. The rationale for this linkage not made explicit.	The emphasis on linguistic correctness and grammar could lead to a mechanistic approach in the teaching of writing. Identifying key linguistic features of written genres should complement 'process' oriented approaches to the teaching of writing.

Genre theory (e.g. Kress 1982, Christie 1984, Martin 1985).	Pupils need to be taught the different characteristics of written genres, and their purposes. Pupils need to be taught how to write different genres, particularly non-fiction forms.	No explicit model of progression in writing, except in terms of 'mastery' of writing different genres.	Genre theory has made explicit the link between purpose, form and audience in the teaching of writing, particularly in the NC for English (e.g. DfEE/QCA 1999:39), and in the National Literacy Strategy.	The views of Kress and Martin that some genres are intrinsically 'powerful', and that mastery of non-fiction forms will enable pupils to change society are naive (Barrs 1994: 252).	Teachers should use linguistic/grammatical analysis to identify priorities in the teaching of writing.
The National Curriculum for English (DfEE/QCA 1999). Stages 1 to 4.	Programmes of Study identify the types of writing that pupils should be taught at Key Stages 1 to 4.	Attainment Targets (1–8) provide a linear pathway or ladder which describe pupils' progress in writing as they move through the key stages.	The National Literacy Strategy has adapted the model of progression in the NC to provide a more prescriptive approach to the teaching of writing in each year across Key Stages 1 to 3.	The levels are often unclear or confusing. Their main function is for summative assessment. It is difficult to use the levels for formative assessment in the classroom, unless they are broken down into smaller steps or discrete skills. The relationship between the levels and the Programmes of Study is conceptually flawed (Wiliam 2001).	

There are two main points to be made about the theories or models of writing analysed in Table 2.2. First, most of these theories have not had a lasting impact on the teaching and assessment of writing, though they have influenced theory and/or practice in the short term (e.g. Britton's theory of writing functions, or the National Writing Project). On the other hand, genre theory and work on the uses of meta-cognition (for example) have contributed to the approaches advocated in the NLS for the teaching of writing. Second, the theories or models summarised in Table 2.2 do not, on the whole, attempt to conceptualise progression in writing. This is because progression is a curriculum concept, linked to specific ideas about what pupils should be capable of achieving as they move through the educational system, though one of the central issues is how closely the levels or stages (however they are defined) should be linked to age. We can conclude that these theories have not contributed significantly to the conceptualisation of progression in the National Curriculum.

As a classroom teacher, I would argue that the ways most teachers of English teach writing, particularly at secondary school, involve a repertoire of approaches drawn from a range of theories or models (whether the teacher is aware of this or not), personal experiences at school or college, and interactions with other colleagues.

A seamless garment or the Emperor's new clothes?

What bearing do these reflections on progression have on the National Curriculum? In a critique of the assessment framework in the National Curriculum, Wiliam has argued that one of the central problems with the conceptualisation of progression is the relationship between the attainment targets and the programmes of study (Wiliam 2001). For example, the fact that the test results are based on different programmes of study rather than the attainment targets, means (according to Wiliam) that the test results are not comparable across the key stages:

> We therefore have key stage 2 tests that are based on the key stage 2 programmes of study and key stage 3 tests based on the key stage 3 programmes of study. The fact that these programmes of study are different means that comparing the results at key stage 3 with those at key stage 2 makes no more sense than saying that a student must have got worse because they achieved a grade C at GCSE and then a grade E at A level in a particular subject.
>
> (Wiliam 2001: 15)

This lack of comparability might explain why the Key Stage 2 test results and teacher assessments were of little use to teachers of Year 7 students, as shown by my research and the research of others (e.g. Sutherland *et al.* 1996, Doyle and Herrington 1998). This was regardless of the practical difficulties of transferring this information and disseminating it to the appropriate staff at the secondary school. My findings about teachers' attitudes to the teaching of writing confirmed Wiliam's general point that the levels do not provide enough data to enable the teacher in Year 7 to judge where the new pupil is at in terms of knowledge and skills. Furthermore, the teacher is not able to plan the Year 7 curriculum on the basis of the Key Stage 2 levels alone. We may conclude that the conceptualisation of progression in the National Curriculum is not a seamless garment, at least not across the key stages. What are the implications for children's writing at transition?

To gain a better understanding of what happens to children's writing skills as they move from the primary to the secondary school, we need to ask three questions. First, what types of writing do pupils (typically) produce in upper primary and lower secondary school classrooms? Second, what expectations of pupils' writing skills do teachers have at transition? Third, what are pupils' experiences and expectations of writing as they move to the secondary school? .

Types of writing in Year 6 and Year 7

OFSTED reports in the last five or six years have continued to highlight the fact that pupils' writing at Key Stage 2 tends to lag behind their reading, and speaking and listening skills (e.g. OFSTED 1999a, 2002). Research in the 1990s found that primary school pupils were not given many openings to read or write, or 'to look critically upon their reading or writing with adults or peers, as a regular and integral part of the teaching and learning process' (Webster *et al.* 1996: 82). The introduction of the National Literacy Strategy was clearly intended to address such concerns.

The evidence suggests that writing in upper primary and lower secondary classrooms is limited to a few main types or genres, and that this has not changed much since the introduction of the National Curriculum. Research in the 1980s in English and Scottish schools identified copying, answering questions, summarising and writing narrative as the most frequently occurring activities (e.g. Martin *et al.* 1976; Gubb *et al.* 1987; Spencer 1984). Looking at the tasks set for Year 7 pupils across the curriculum as they started at the secondary school, Galton commented on the limited and repetitive nature of the work which pupils did in most subjects, with an emphasis on note-taking, copying diagrams and 'doing written work' (Galton and Willcocks 1983: 167). In their follow-up study 20 years later, Hargreaves and Galton argued that in spite of the introduction of the National Curriculum, the curriculum and much of the teaching had remained largely unchanged (Hargreaves and Galton 2002: xvi).

Secondary teachers' attitudes and expectations

With respect to teachers' attitudes and expectations of pupils' writing skills at the transition between Years 6 and 7, there has been limited research. I will summarise the main points with reference to the core curriculum subjects, as well as history and geography.

In general secondary teachers, particularly teachers of English, expect new pupils to have competence in basic writing skills, though they feel that this is often not the case in reality. For example, Sutherland's study, while in part reflecting specific features of the Northern Ireland educational system (e.g. the retention of the 11+ exam), described the perceptions of secondary teachers and their pupils about writing at transition. About a third of the English teachers interviewed by Sutherland considered that the writing of paragraphs had not been mastered at primary school, and deduced that this skill had not been taught properly. Sustained writing (i.e. essays) was considered to be difficult for new pupils, though the study did not describe how this skill was taught at secondary school. Newspaper reports, keeping journals, drafting and redrafting a piece of work and the use of word processors were each reported to be unfamiliar to many pupils entering one or more of the post-primary schools (Sutherland *et al.* 1996: 44).

The types of writing most pupils were expected to produce in English lessons at the beginning of secondary school tended to be autobiographical or stories. Of the secondary teachers interviewed, most considered that essays and 'extended writing' were the activities that pupils liked least in English (*ibid.*: 153).

The other concerns or expectations of English teachers about writing included:

- scepticism about the way editing and redrafting skills were taught in the 'other' phase, and the lack of agreement between the phases about the best ways of doing this (e.g. Suffolk LEA 1996: 14, 17);
- the importance of correct punctuation, sentence construction and paragraphing for Year 7 pupils. Many teachers hoped that new

pupils in Year 7 would be able 'to write fluently and legibly and at speed, and respond to questions with whole sentences' (e.g. Schagen and Kerr 1999: 42–44).

- the Key Stage 2 test provided a model for primary English teaching (mainly comprehensions and creative writing) that was different from that encountered at secondary school, with its emphasis on the study of literature (Marshall and Brindley 1998: 133). The authors argued that it was difficult for primary and secondary teachers to communicate cross-phase when they had different models of what constituted English.

Although recent research does not include data on teachers' attitudes to the teaching and uses of writing in mathematics at transition, there are some findings about science. There were concerns that new pupils to the secondary school did not know how to structure science reports, or copy instructions accurately (e.g. Sutherland *et al.* 1996: 126–127), and that poor writing skills were a more serious obstacle to pupils' progress in secondary school science than their lack of understanding of scientific concepts (*ibid.*:176). The report of the Suffolk LEA indicated that there was more discussion of science at Key Stages 1 and 2, and usually more emphasis on written work at secondary school, though the approaches used to teach pupils the formal writing up of experimental work were not described (Suffolk LEA 1996: 30–31).

In history and geography there was also a lack of communication between primary and secondary teachers about the teaching and uses of writing, with a tendency among some secondary teachers to criticise the primary schools for not teaching the writing types that would be needed at Key Stages 3 and 4 (e.g. Huggins and Knight 1997: 341; Schagen and Kerr 1999: 43). We can conclude from this section that there was often a lack of cross-phase communication between teachers about the teaching and uses of writing, and the types of writing skills that new pupils would need to be successful learners in Year 7.

Pupils' experiences and expectations

In this section I consider the core curriculum subjects, and history and geography. Research suggests that pupils are sensitive to similarities and differences in the teaching and uses of writing in Years 6 and 7, while several studies reported higher levels of enjoyment of English at the secondary school (e.g. Sutherland *et al.* 1996: 158; Suffolk LEA 1996:14–15). There were more opportunities to write about literature in Year 7, which reflected the different nature of 'English' as a subject at secondary school. Writing – especially 'long essays' and 'long home-works' – was identified as the least liked aspect of English, though a few pupils said they enjoyed writing stories or poems. Other types of writing, such as scripts and designing a trailer for a film, were much more popular (Sutherland *et al.* 1996: 159), while Schagen and Kerr found that the main difference in English in Year 7 was the emphasis on creative writing (Schagen and Kerr 1999: 44), a finding similar to that reported by Gubb and colleagues in 1987.

However, a different picture emerged from the research conducted by Marshall and Brindley (1998) in two west London schools and one Oxfordshire school. At the end of Year 6 the pupils gave a picture of primary English in which story writing was the main creative activity (Marshall and Brindley 1998: 128). They also emphasised the importance of writing skills, e.g. spelling, punctuation, paragraphs, etc. At the end of Year 7, the pupils' clearest sense of progression was expressed in terms of their written work. They all felt that their work was 'more detailed' and 'more thorough', and they felt they had more time to edit and redraft their own stories, using a wider range of 'describing words'. (Marshall and Brindley 1998: 129–130). It may be that the differences in these studies were due to differences between the schools.

The most common response from pupils about writing in science was that at secondary school they had to write 'more detailed and better structured reports', as opposed to the 'story-type' form used at primary school. However, in some primary schools pupils had also written structured reports of experiments, though other pupils reported completing worksheets after an experiment in primary and secondary school. There was thus no uniformity of experience in the writing expected of pupils in science as they moved from primary to secondary school (Sutherland *et al.* 1996: 136). Pupils' main complaints focused on the amount of writing in secondary school science, and the degree of detail required (*ibid.*:137). Other research studies reported pupils' views that there was too much copying (Schagen and Kerr 1999: 45) and excessive note-taking (Jarman 1993: 24–25) in Year 7 science lessons.

Where secondary history was concerned, Schagen and Kerr commented that many pupils in Year 7 found it difficult,

> given the amount of reading and writing involved, as well as the amount of vocabulary that has to be understood, and dates, names and events remembered. Some were disappointed to find that there was little opportunity to continue in-depth topic and project work.
>
> (Schagen and Kerr 1999: 45)

The different nature of the writing demands made on pupils in Year 7 was not analysed in further detail. There was no research evidence about pupils' perceptions of writing in geography in Years 6 or 7.

So what are we to conclude? This section demonstrates that there is little sense of continuity in pupils' accounts of writing in Years 6 and 7. Furthermore, the research evidence shows that the majority of writing activities in primary and secondary classrooms is still restricted to a few types, and that this has not changed appreciably in the last 20 years. Over several decades, a lack of continuity and progression has persisted in spite of the introduction of the National Curriculum. This book will attempt to explain why.

Implications for the practising teacher

There are a number of simple, practical steps one could take at the beginning of Year 7 to ensure pupils make a good start. For example:

- ask new pupils to bring their best piece of work (or the piece they are most proud of) from Year 5 or 6 to their first English lesson in Year 7. This could be put in their National Curriculum folder or exercise book, and used as a marker for the assignments they produce, particularly in their first term at secondary school. It is a very good way of raising pupils' expectations at the beginning of Key Stage 3 – their work in Year 7 has got to be better than in Year 6![1]
- ask pupils to bring one or more personal targets from the end of Year 6 (in English, mathematics and science) to their first lesson in Year 7. They should share the target(s) with a partner and the teacher, and write the target(s) in the front of their exercise book;
- discuss with pupils in class what they have done in Year 6 (or earlier), within the context of a topic, theme, or skills that might be developed in class, so that they can see that you value their experiences at primary school;
- use reading logs or journals for private reading from Year 6 at the start of Year 7. Primary and secondary teachers need to agree on the types of response they expect from their pupils, so that the use of reading logs creates opportunities for progression in Year 7;

1 I am indebted to Tim Brighouse for this suggestion.

- conduct one-to-one reviews with pupils in Year 7 on a termly basis. Use their best work from primary school and Year 6 targets when discussing their progress at secondary school. Time needs to be made available by the school for individual reviews and target-setting, otherwise it will not happen;
- use CATs scores to predict students' potential, and to track their progress through Year 7 and the rest of Key Stage 3, even though my experience as a teacher suggests that CATs scores are not always reliable guides to pupils' future achievements, particularly where extended writing is concerned.

3 Bridges or chasms?
Children's writing at primary–secondary transition

> 'And how many hours a day did you do lessons?' said Alice, in a hurry to change the subject.
> 'Ten hours the first day,' said the Mock Turtle, 'nine the next, and so on.'
> 'What a curious plan!' exclaimed Alice.
> 'That's the reason they're called lessons,' the Gryphon remarked, 'because they lessen from day to day.'
> *Alice's Adventures in Wonderland*, Chapter 9.

Introduction

The view of the curriculum given by the Mock Turtle and the Gryphon challenged all of Alice's preconceptions about the nature of education. A curriculum plan in which the number of lessons decreased every day would not, in most quarters, be regarded as facilitating pupils' progress, though it gave the Mock Turtle and the Gryphon additional time for extra-curricular activities, such as games and dances, about which they were most enthusiastic. We never learn whether they made comparable progress in academic subjects such as 'reeling and writhing'.

Much attention has been focused in recent years on the lack of progress or regression that occurs in many pupils' achievements at Key Stage 3, compared with their progress at Key Stage 2. The dip at the beginning of Year 7 is considered to be symptomatic of repetitive and boring teaching that does not build on pupils' achievements in Year 6; according to some research this state of affairs has not changed significantly since the introduction of the National Curriculum (e.g. Hargreaves and Galton 2002: xvi). If we consider children's experiences and perceptions of writing at the end of Year 6 and during the first half of Year 7, does my evidence support these widely publicised views?

The argument in this chapter, based on my case study, is that the writing that pupils did at the end of Year 6 and at the beginning of Year 7 was restricted to a few types, though these types were not the same at the different points in time when I sampled the pupils' work. There was little evidence of planned continuity in the types of writing that pupils did as they moved from Year 6 to Year 7; some evidence of unplanned continuity and progression (in history); and considerable evidence of regression in the majority of types of writing that pupils used during the first term of Year 7. In general, the pupils I tracked tended to use their existing repertoire of writing skills (acquired in Year 6) during their first year at the secondary school. The possible reasons for this regression in the pupils' writing, and its significance for raising standards at Key Stage 3, will be discussed below.

At Jeremy Priestley School (the secondary school) the four 'target' pupils were taught in their mixed-ability tutor groups; Lauren and Zoe were in different tutor groups, while James and Gavin were in the same group, so some of the differences between the pupils reflected the fact that they had different teachers. The writing types that the two boys produced were broadly similar, but not identical, and the number of each writing type was usually different. This suggests that these two pupils responded differently to the same instructions; their understanding of and response to a task were often different.

The pupils' perceptions of their writing experiences were that two or three writing activities predominated during the first term of Year 7 – mainly answering questions and copying, and that more copying took place in Year 7 than at the end of Year 6. Their views about what constituted 'good' writing tended to emphasise technical accuracy and neatness, though not exclusively. These opinions were based on the categories that were used by their teacher in Year 6, particularly as the pupils prepared for the end-of-key stage tests.

My findings about writing thus tend to support more general statements about the regression experienced by some pupils at the beginning of Year 7, though I think it is a mistake simply to 'blame the teachers'. The picture is in fact a very complex one, and by looking in more detail at what was 'going on' in terms of the uses and teaching of writing in this and the next three chapters, I shall identify some of the contradictory pressures on pupils and their teachers at transition. I consider in detail the types of writing that the pupils did during three 'snapshot' weeks: towards the end of Year 6, and during the first and second halves of the autumn term in Year 7. I also analyse the perceptions of the pupils about the types of writing they did, based on their writing logs and interviews. Many of the main points in the next section are summarised in Table 3.1 through to Table 3.3.

The pupils' writing in the snapshot weeks

The main argument of this section is that, from the evidence of the snapshot weeks, there was little or no continuity or progression in the pupils' writing from the end of Year 6 through to the end of the autumn term in Year 7. There was virtually no similarity between the types of writing done towards the end of Year 6, compared to the types of writing done in Year 7.

Table 3.1 shows the different types of writing identified from the pupils' workbooks during the three snapshot weeks. Identifying the most frequently occurring types of writing does not indicate the relative time spent on different writing activities, nor does it directly enlarge our understanding of the ways that writing was taught. These questions will be dealt with in Chapter 4. However, such an analysis

Table 3.1 Different types of writing identified during the three snapshot weeks

Type of writing	W/b 23 June	W/b 22 September	W/b 1 December
Answer questions	9	6	17
Brainstorm			3
Cartoon		1	2
Cloze		1	3
Definitions		6	4
Discussions			
Explanations	1	4	5
Graph		2	1
Labels	2	8	11
Letter		1	
List	1	6	7
Narrative	8	1	1
Newspaper			
Notes	2		
Other	1	2	1
Persuasion			
Poem	4		
Procedures			1
Recount		5	2
Report	2	2	2
Script	1		
Story		1	2
Summary	3	1	
Table or chart		9	7
Totals	34	56	69

does indicate whether certain writing activities predominated across the curriculum. For example, in the week beginning 23 June 1997 (in Year 6), 34 instances of writing were identified, and of these the most frequently occurring types were answering questions (26.5%), and narrative (23.5%), together these two types of writing accounted for almost half the writing that the pupils did. Answering questions occurred most frequently in English and RS (8/9 times). The category of narrative included newspaper reports, TV news reports and diaries, but the writing did not show much differentiation into different genres; the examples were forms of narrative writing, as will be discussed in more detail below.

The target pupils were in the same class, but they did not all produce the same types of written work. They all wrote a poem, but either they did different tasks within a subject or were at different stages of (say) topic work on the Victorians. There were no obvious differences between the types of writing produced by the pupils that could be linked to gender, though there were some differences in content that appeared to reflect gender, e.g. James wrote a report about the army for his Victorian project, while Lauren wrote about clothes.

The first snapshot week at the secondary school (week beginning 22 September, the third week of the autumn term) revealed a different pattern of writing activity. Fifty-six instances of writing were identified, and there were 16 different types of writing. The larger number of subjects at secondary school, and an increase in curriculum time (from 23.5 to 25 hours per week) may account for the increase in the amount of writing and the number of types of writing. The most frequently occurring categories were: completing a table or chart (16.1%), labelling a picture or diagram (14.3%), answering questions (10.7%), writing or copying definitions (10.7%), making a list (10.7%) and recounts (8.9%). These six types of writing accounted for 71.4% of the different types of writing identified. At first glance this suggest a noticeable difference in the types of writing that the target pupils did in the target week at primary school, compared to the first snapshot week at the secondary school, though answering questions featured prominently in both samples of work. It should also be noted that the writing types identified in the secondary snapshot weeks were present in the children's writing in Year 6, spread through the year.

The distribution of the most frequently occurring types of writing according to subject in the first snapshot week at the secondary school (Table 3.2) shows that tables or charts were most frequently used in the pupils' writing in mathematics and religious studies (RS). For example, labelling occurred most frequently in modern foreign languages and geography, while answering questions occurred most frequently in modern foreign languages. Lists were made in languages and PSVE, while definitions occurred most frequently in RS and mathematics. This shows that the statements about the frequency of different types of writing have to take into account variations across the curriculum, and though the sample was small, this preliminary analysis raises questions about teaching and learning styles, and the uses of writing in the delivery of the secondary curriculum.

The differences between the pupils' written work in the snapshot week beginning 23 June (Year 6) and the week beginning 23 September (Year 7) does not mean that progression in writing had taken place in the autumn term of secondary school, unless one can identify an improvement or 'building on' in the way the pupils wrote (for example) newspaper front pages or science reports. Examples of children's writing from Year 6 and Year 7 will be discussed below, so that some comparisons can be made about the ways the target pupils tackled similar writing tasks in primary and secondary school. However, one could argue that the increase in the number of writing types identified in the snapshot weeks (from 11 to 16) represented a form of progression, though this may be linked to the increased number of subjects at secondary school.

In the second snapshot week at the secondary school (week beginning 1 December) the most frequently occurring categories of writing were answering questions (24.6%), labelling (15.9%), completing a table or chart (10.1%) and making a list (10.1%). These four categories accounted for 60.8 per cent of the types of writing identified in this week.

There was a greater similarity in the types of writing undertaken in the two snapshot weeks at the secondary school, than between the snapshot week in Year 6 and the week beginning 22 September in Year 7. Answering questions, labelling, making a list, and completing a table or chart occurred frequently in both secondary snapshot weeks compared to other types of writing, though answering questions showed an increase in frequency in the second secondary snapshot week. The snapshot weeks suggest that certain types of writing predominated across the secondary curriculum, but with the exception of poetry and recounts, they did not include clearly identifiable fiction or non-fiction genres.

The distribution of types of writing across the second secondary snapshot week showed similarities and differences with the week beginning 22 September (Table 3.3). Answering questions was used most frequently by the target pupils in mathematics, history, modern

Table 3.2 Distribution of the most frequently occurring types of writing in the snapshot week beginning 22 September at Jeremy Priestley School

Type of writing	English	Maths	Science	History	Geography	RS	MFL	PSVE	Totals
Answers	1	1	1						6
Definitions		2				3	3		6
Label		1		1	3		3		8
List			1		1	1	2	2	6
Table/chart		4	1			3			9

Table 3.3 Distribution of the most frequently occurring types of writing in the snapshot week beginning 1 December at Jeremy Priestley School

Type of writing	English	Maths	Science	History	Geography	RS	MFL	Drama	Music	PSVE	Totals
Answers	1	5		3		3	4	1			17
Label		5	3	1			2				11
List			1				3			3	7
Table/chart		3	2						1	1	7

foreign languages (French and German) and religious studies, and it may be that the pupils were being tested on what they knew at this point in the term. They used labelling, and charts or tables, mainly in mathematics and science, while lists were written most frequently in modern foreign languages and PSVE.

Categories and concepts

It is also necessary to elaborate on some of the dominant categories identified above, in particular 'labelling', and 'completing a table or chart', because they can mean different things in different contexts. For example, labelling occurs when a pupil labels a timeline with information about the Romans or important events in his/her own life, in an account of a science experiment when a diagram of the apparatus is labelled; in mathematics it is when different polygons are named. The notion of labelling can cover a variety of tasks, and identifying the type of writing using this general term does not indicate the cognitive nature of the task which the pupil undertook. The cognitive challenge of (for example) labelling your own timeline involves understanding what a timeline is, and how it can be used to communicate information about yourself. This is a different type of cognitive activity from labelling a diagram of a bunsen burner.

Charts and tables are used to classify information into different categories, and then to establish (in a visually effective manner) similarities and differences between the categories. This chapter contains several examples of tables or charts used in this manner. The identification of the written product (e.g. a table or chart, or an example of labelling) does not indicate the cognitive nature of the task that led to it. The contexts in which writing took place will be considered in Chapter 4, focusing on examples of the teaching and uses of writing in the classroom. However, a preliminary finding from the analysis of the secondary snapshot weeks is that most types of writing were used to develop or test understanding, but did not involve the teaching of writing per se. The pupils may well have made progress in their knowledge and understanding of different subjects by December of their first term of Year 7, though this cannot be proved from my data. The evidence from their exercise books shows that similar types of writing were used in the first and second halves of the autumn term of Year 7; progression did not occur in the development of the pupils' writing.

Examples of children's writing

In this section I argue that the writing the pupils produced in four different genres in Years 6 and 7 showed evidence of regression and a lack of continuity. The genres I will analyse are: newspapers, science reports, letters and stories, because they are typical of the sorts of writing that pupils produce in Year 7, though I will refer to other types of writing as well.

Most of the examples of the pupils' writing which I discuss below could be marked as weak Level 4 (or in some cases on the borderline between Levels 3 and 4). The levels do not, in my opinion, do justice to the differences and similarities between the texts, so I have provided a more detailed commentary on the significant features of the pupils' writing. The processes of teaching and learning which generated the pupils' writing will be described in Chapter 5.

Newspapers

Though the pupils produced newspaper front pages in Years 6 and 7, the examples of their work (analysed below) showed little evidence of continuity or progression, in terms of layout, structure or language. Figures 3.1 and 3.2 show examples of newspapers based on the Victorian topic in Year 6, by Gavin and Lauren. The newspaper front pages have similar generic features: the name of the paper, a headline, date, issue number and price. The reports are set out in columns, and start in the present tense.

When I interviewed the pupils at the primary school they identified writing in the present tense, and setting the articles out in columns, as being the main features of a newspaper report, unlike a story, which (as Gavin explained) was written 'across the page'.

I could not find newspaper reports written by either Gavin or Lauren in Year 7, but I found two by Zoe, though neither had been written during the two secondary snapshot weeks. Figure 3.3 is part of a newspaper report written in history in the spring term 1998 about the death of Thomas à Becket. I have no data about how the pupils were prepared for this task. The front page has the name of the paper, or maybe it is the headline 'New News', the date and '5 straken' (the cost?) at the top of the page. There is a sketched picture, labelled 'Church', and the report starts 'The news we bring you today is Thomas Becket has died', showing the same emphasis on topicality ('today') as in the Year 6 front pages. The rest of the report is narrative, an account based on or copied out of a history book. Columns are not used; there is no

THE Royal
Archbishop
Chants Victoria
as queen

20th June 1837 No. 25 London ____ 5 Shillings

Today is the day when victoria (because)
becomes our queen. She also 1837 and that
we can't believe it learned how to is today she
it's fabulous we have play the piano will marry her
all traced victorias and was taught german cousin
life and she had the
most wonderful life. She
was a lonely child when
she was young and
she lived in Kensington
palace with her mother.
Our young queen didn't
have to go to school
because her mum was   how to draw.   in the future.
German so she hired This is totally   It was only
a German governess, fantastic she wasn't this morning—
and she also learned aloud to be alone continue on
french, History and arithmetic until 20th June the next page.

Figure 3.1 Gavin's newspaper front page (Year 6)

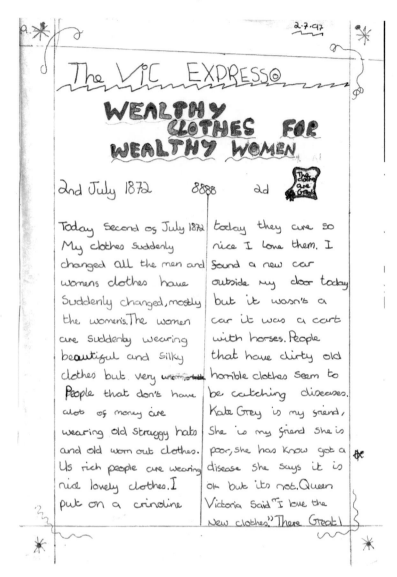

The VIC EXPRESSO

WEALTHY CLOTHES FOR WEALTHY WOMEN

2nd July 1872   8888   2d

Today Second os July 1872 My clothes Suddenly changed all the men and womens clothes have Suddenly changed, mostly the women's. The women are Suddenly wearing beautiful and Silky clothes but very ~~wom~~ People that don't have alot of money are wearing old Struggy hats and old worn out clothes. Us rich people are wearing nice lovely clothes. I put on a crinoline today they are so nice I love them. I Sound a new car outside my door today but it wasn't a car it was a cart with horses. People that have dirty old horrible clothes Seem to be catching diseases. Kate Grey is my sriend, She is my sriend She is poor, she has know got a disease She says it is ok but its not. Queen Victoria Said "I love the New clothes." There Great!

Figure 3.2 Lauren's newspaper front page (Year 6)

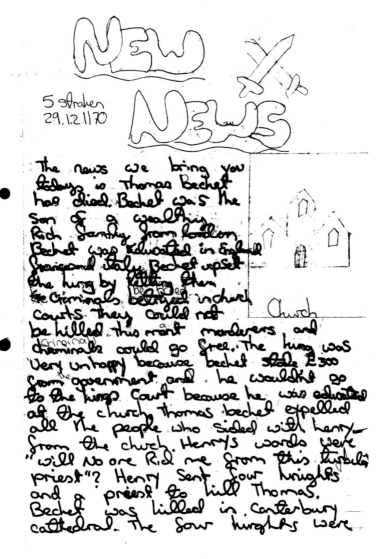

Figure 3.3 Zoe's newspaper front page in history (Year 7)

paragraphing, and capital letters at the beginning of sentences or proper names are sometimes omitted. The report, covering over one and a half sides of A4 paper contains more information that the Year 6 newspapers, but it shows less awareness of the conventions that should be used when writing a front page.

In English Zoe started drafting a front page based on a play in which some children had broken into a laboratory (Figure 3.4). Her draft report contains the name of the paper 'The World's New's'(sic), the price and a headline 'School Brake in'. The report tries to convey a sense of immediacy by starting 'There was terrible new's last night at the Stevens school of tropical diseses three children broke in by getting over the barbed wire fence. . .'. Paragraphing and columns were not used, the language was a bit repetitive (e.g. the two uses of 'gratefull'), and she used the apostrophe incorrectly.

These examples show that the pupils were writing newspaper front pages in history in Years 6 and 7. The intention was to convey information about historical events in a different form and in a more immediate manner. The same intention is evident in the draft report in Zoe's Year 7 English exercise book. In Year 7 the pupils appeared to be using the knowledge they had acquired in primary school about writing newspaper reports, and these examples suggest that there was no progression in the terms of structure or the language used.

Science reports

There was no evidence of progression in the ways the pupils were expected to write up reports of science experiments in Years 6 and 7, though there was progression in terms of the knowledge and concepts that the pupils acquired in Year 7. The pupils used a structured approach when writing up experiments in Year 6, using headings provided by the teacher. For example, in Year 6 Zoe's draft of an experiment on air pressure (Figure 3.5) is divided into three sections: Prediction, Method, and Diagrams and Results. The report is written in the first person, and the final section contains an explanation. James also drafted his report; the teacher corrected one spelling mistake, and requested a diagram. Figure 3.6 shows the final version of his report, including his explanation of the results.

In Year 6 different headings were used to structure reports of experiments that were part of other topics. For example, in Figure 3.7 James wrote up an experiment on taste as part of a project on 'Food and Farming' using the headings Procedure, Equipment, Diagram and Results. In an experiment on how much salt can dissolve in water, the

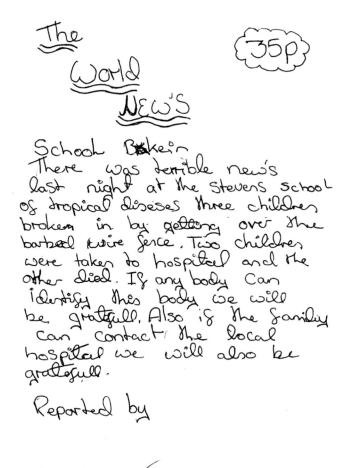

Figure 3.4 Zoe's draft newspaper report in English (Year 7)

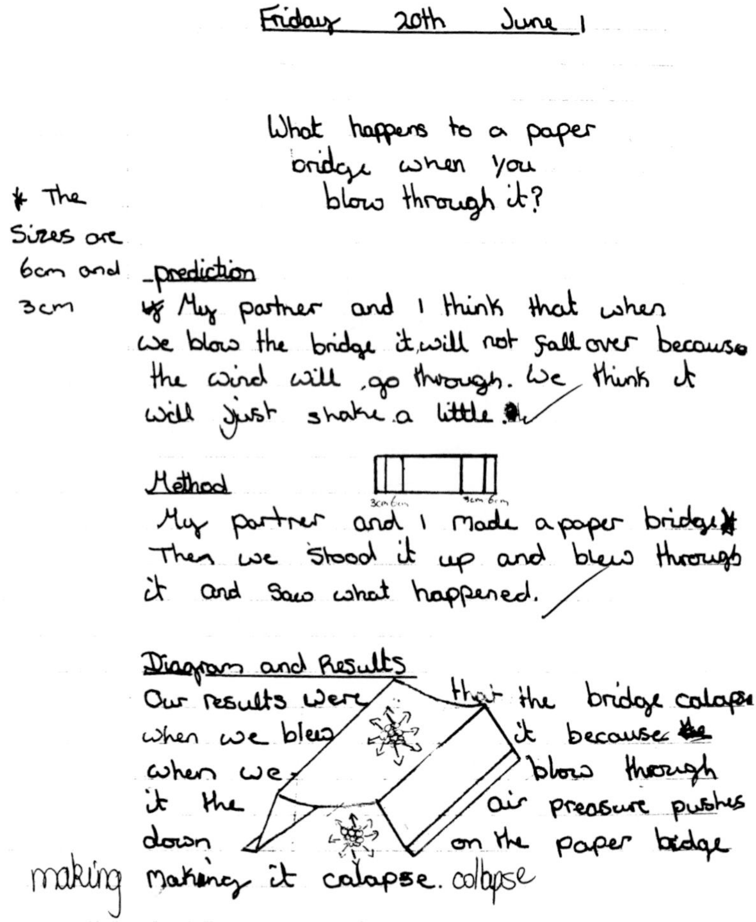

Friday   20th   June 1

What happens to a paper
bridge when you
blow through it?

✱ The
Sizes are
6cm and
3cm

prediction

✱ My partner and I think that when
we blow the bridge it will not fall over because
the wind will go through. We think it
will just shake a little. ✱

Method

My partner and I made a paper bridge ✱
Then we stood it up and blew through
it and saw what happened.

Diagram and Results

Our results were   that the bridge colapse
when we blew   it because the
when we   blow through
it the   air preasure pushes
down   on the paper bridge
making making it colapse. colapse

Figure 3.5 Zoe's draft report on air pressure (Year 6)

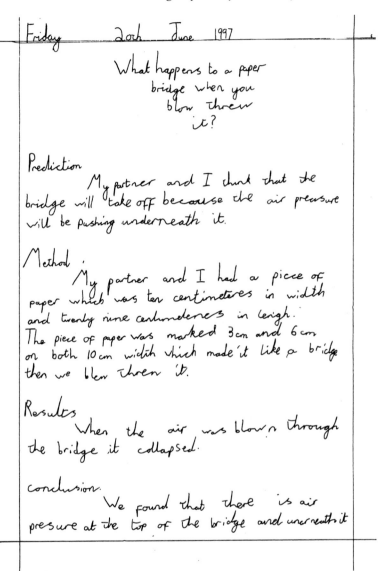

Friday   20th   June   1997

What happens to a paper
bridge when you
blow threw
it?

Prediction
My partner and I think that the
bridge will take off because the air preasure
will be pushing underneath it.

Method
My partner and I had a piece of
paper which was ten centimetres in width
and twenty nine centimeteres in lengh.
The piece of paper was marked 3cm and 6cm
on both 10cm width which made it like a bridge
then we blew thren it.

Results
When the air was blown through
the bridge it collapsed.

conclusion.
We found that there is air
presure at the top of the bridge and unerneath it

Figure 3.6 James's final report on the experiment on air pressure (Year 6)
(continued overleaf)

Friday   20th June 1997

When we blew the air presure was pushed out from undernieth so the top air presure pushed it down and it collapsed.

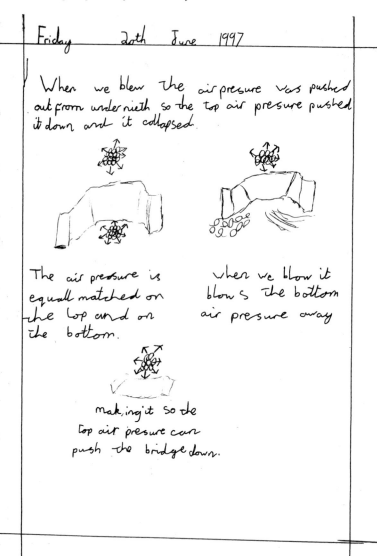

The air pressure is equall matched on the top and on the bottom.

when we blow it blows the bottom air presure away

making it so the top air presure can push the bridge down.

Figure 3.6 (continued)

Tuesday 28th. January 1997

Taste Experiment.

Procedure.

We used our lolypop stick to dip into the sugar water to see where we could taste it on our toungs, we did this also with vinigar tea and salt, then we had to draw a tounge to show where we could taste it.

Equipment

Cups, Lolypop sticks, Vinigar, salt, tea, sugar, water, paper, pens and paper towls.

Diagram

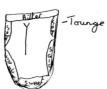

Results.

We tasted sour and salty things on the side of our toungs sweet at the front and bitter at the back

Conclusion

I discovered that different parts of the tounge taste different things

Figure 3.7 James's experiment on taste (Year 6)

first two headings were questions: 'What equipment will I need?' and 'What do I need to measure?', followed by 'Method' (five numbered sentences, each starting 'we will. . .'), and 'Results'.

In Year 7 there were more opportunities to do experiments, and the pupils said that was one of the things they had looked forward to at secondary school. They were expected to know how to write up their experiments in a structured manner, but often a narrative account (i.e. recount) was acceptable if it demonstrated understanding. There was some variation between science teachers in Year 7 in terms of how the experiments should be written up. For example, the most structured report in James's science exercise book was at the beginning of the autumn term (Figure 3.8), using the headings 'Method', 'Results' and 'Conclusion', and written in the first person. The next experiment, on using bunsen burners, was written as a narrative, as were most of the subsequent reports, including those written during the snapshot week beginning 1 December. The teacher had corrected a spelling mistake in each report.

Zoe had a different science teacher in Year 7, and the experiments in her exercise book contained more labelled diagrams of equipment, copied definitions, and results presented in tabular form. For example, the experiment conducted during the first secondary snapshot week (w/b 22 September) 'Making water indicator paper' contains a labelled diagram, three pieces of indicator paper, and a table of the results (Figure 3.9). Later on in the term, in November, an experiment with filter paper used statements as headings with question marks ('What we did with the filter paper?'; 'What happened?'), an approach similar to that used sometimes in Year 6 (e.g. Figure 3.6).

The typical examples reproduced here show that the pupils were learning new concepts and acquiring a richer technical vocabulary in Year 7 science, (e.g. 'Bunsen burner', 'filtration', 'evaporation', etc). This suggests that progression was taking place in terms of knowledge and understanding during the autumn term of Year 7. However there was little or no progression in the ways science reports were written in Years 6 and 7; if anything the evidence presented suggests regression.

Letters

This section shows that there was no progression and little continuity in the ways the pupils wrote letters in Year 7, when compared to Year 6. The pupils were taught to write formal and informal letters at primary school, and they drew on this knowledge when they were asked to write letters in Year 7. For example, in the spring term of Year 6, as part of

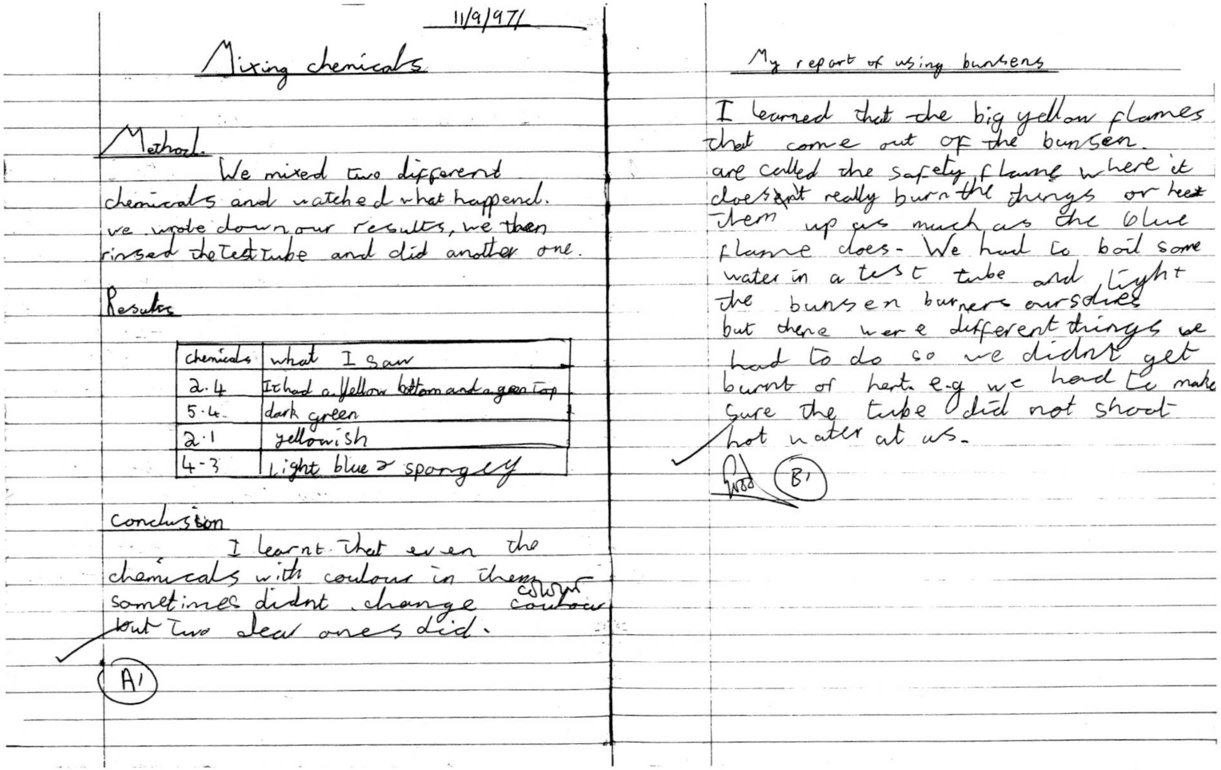

Mixing chemicals

11/9/97

Method

We mixed two different chemicals and watched what happend. We wrote down our results, we then rinsed the test tube and did another one.

Results

chemicals	what I saw
2.4	Itched a yellow bottom and a green top
5.4	dark green
2.1	yellowish
4.3	light blue & sparingly

Conclusion

I learnt that even the chemicals with colours in them sometimes didnt change colour but two clear ones did.

(A')

My report of using bunsens

I learned that the big yellow flames that come out of the bunsen are called the safety flame where it doesn't really burn the things or heat them up as much as the blue flame does. We had to boil some water in a test tube and light the bunsen burner ourselves but there were different things we had to do eg we didnt get burnt of hot eg we had to make sure the tube did not shoot hot water at us.

(A) (B')

Figure 3.8 James's science report at the beginning of Year 7

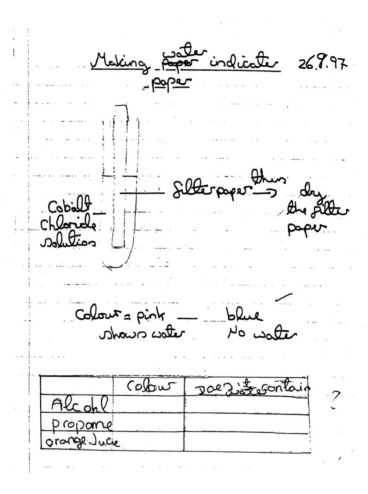

Figure 3.9 Zoe's report on 'Making water indicator paper' (Year 7)

his project on rainforests, James wrote a formal letter to the Association of Agriculture asking for information about the growing of bananas. Figure 3.10 shows the draft of this letter. The formal features he had been taught were setting out the addresses correctly, and the appropriate beginning and ending of the letter. The language is formal and polite, using a conditional verb, e.g. as in the last sentence 'I would be very pleased with whatever you could send me'. This letter was written for a real audience, and James received information as a result for his project.

When I interviewed the pupils in early October in Year 7 we discussed the letter-writing they had done at junior school. James remembered writing this letter, and he explained that he had learned to write a formal letter in Year 5, though he couldn't really remember 'being taught' in detail. Gavin also remembered writing a formal letter to the government about pollution in the rainforests in Year 6; he described this as a 'normal' letter.

A more informal style could be used for other purposes. For example, as part of their study of Greek myths in Year 6, Gavin wrote a postcard from Odysseus describing some of his adventures with the Cyclops (Figure 3.11). Here the purpose was empathetic, and used as a way of demonstrating understanding of the story, combined with some features of the postcard such as the address and a stamp. The message is a retelling of the story, combined with boastful comments by Odysseus which reveal something of his character, e.g. 'Only someone like me would think of such a genius plan'.

In the pupils' writing in Year 7 I could not find an example of a formal letter. One could argue that this demonstrated a lack of continuity, in that the teachers were not extending the use of a genre that had been covered in Year 6. On the other hand, if the Year 7 teachers knew that formal letter writing had been covered in Year 6, and made a conscious decision not to teach it, this could be interpreted as an example of continuity. In fact, my interviews showed that the Year 7 teachers did not have detailed, prior knowledge about the written genres that pupils from different primary schools had been taught, though in some cases secondary teachers discussed with pupils what they had learned in Year 6 (see below).

In English letters were used to demonstrate understanding of a literary text, or were stimulated by the text. For example, during Year 7 the four target pupils read *Two Weeks with the Queen* by Maurice Gleitzman as a class reader. In Zoe's class the pupils were asked to write a letter to the Queen, about a topic that concerned them. The activity was intended as an opportunity for pupils to develop their own ideas,

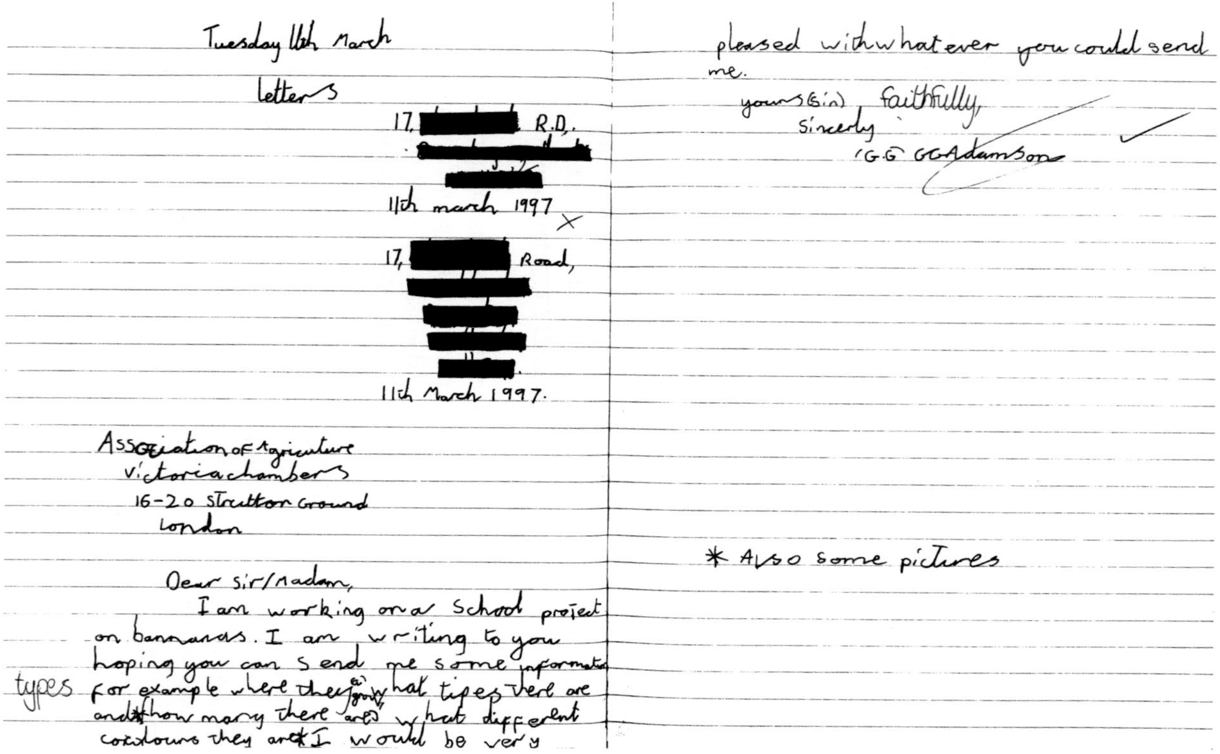

Tuesday 11th March

Letters

17, R.D. ████
████ ██
11th March 1997 ✗

17, ████ Road,
████ ████ ████ ████
11th March 1997.

Association of Agriculture
v. victoria chambers
16-20 Stratton Ground
London

Dear Sir/Madam,

I am working on a school project on bananas. I am writing to you hoping you can send me some information. For example where they grow, what types are there and how many there are and what different colours they are and I would be very ...

... pleased with whatever you could send me.

yours (Sir) faithfully
Sincerely.
G.G. Grahamson

types

* Also some pictures

Figure 3.10 James's draft of a formal letter (Year 6)

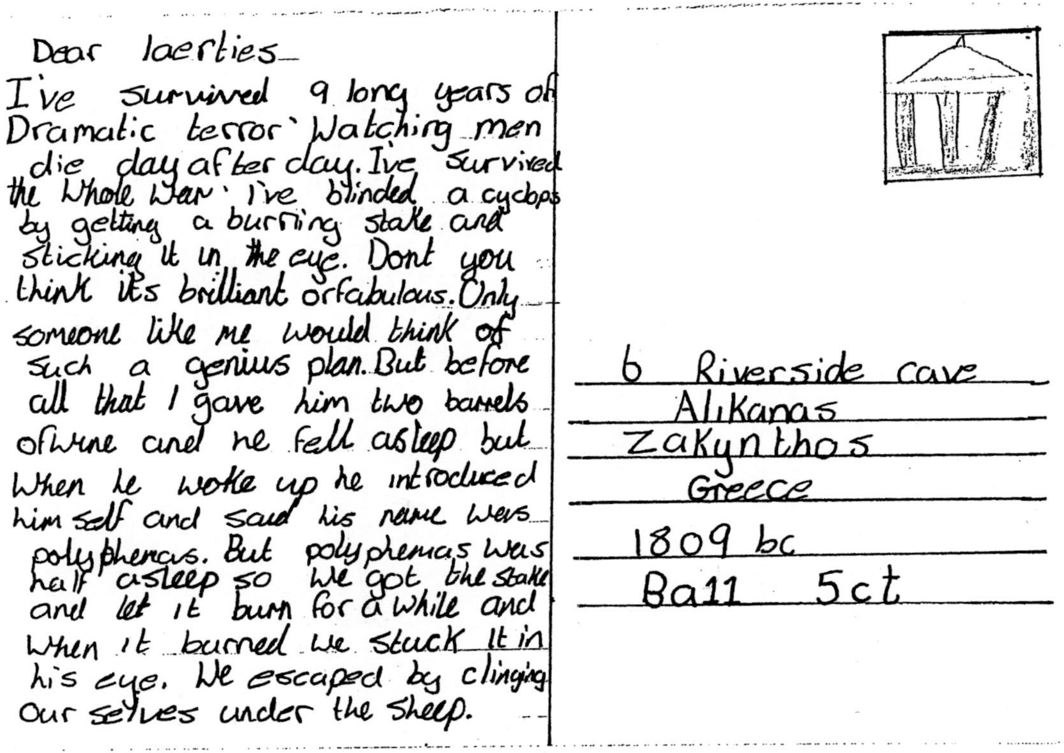

Dear laerties—

I've survived 9 long years of dramatic terror watching men die day after day. I've survived the whole war. I've blinded a cyclops by getting a burning stake and sticking it in the eye. Dont you think its brilliant or fabulous. Only

someone like me would think of such a genius plan. But before all that I gave him two barrels of wine and he fell asleep but

when he woke up he introduced himself and said his name were polyphemos. But polyphemos was half asleep so we got the stake and let it burn for a while and

when it burned we stuck it in his eye. We escaped by clinging our selves under the sheep.

6 Riverside Cave
Alkanas
Zakynthos
Greece
1809 bc
Ba11 5ct

Figure 3.11 Gavin's postcard from Odysseus (Year 6)

rather than an exercise in writing a formal letter. According to Zoe the teacher checked briefly whether the pupils had learned how to set out a letter correctly at primary school before letting them start on the task: 'She (the teacher) asked us if we knew how to write a proper letter, and we said yes, and she said well we can just start then.'

James, Gavin and Lauren were taught English by Mrs Lee, and they all wrote letters to the Queen as if they were Colin (the main character), asking for her help in curing his brother of cancer. The letters by Lauren (Figure 3.12) and Zoe (Figure 3.13) are typical of those produced by the majority of the pupils. The letters are informal in layout and style, though without a date, and contain some spelling and punctuation mistakes. Their main purpose was to demonstrate the pupils' understanding of this part of the story rather than developing writing skills. They do not show progression in terms of form, purpose or cognitive demand, compared to the two examples (Figures 3.10 and 3.11) from Year 6.

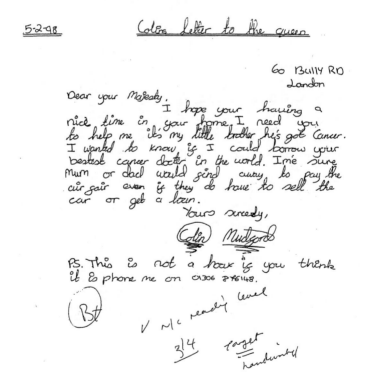

Figure 3.12 Lauren's letter to the Queen (Year 7)

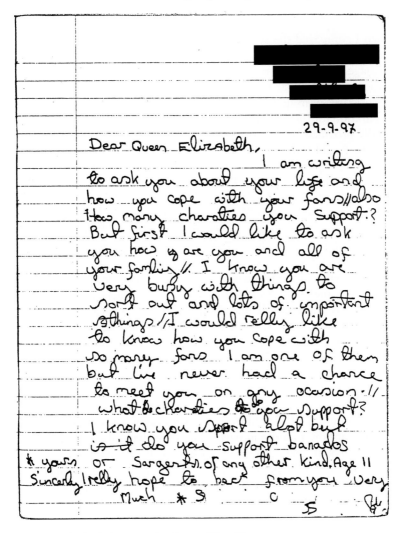

29-9-97

Dear Queen Elizabeth,
I am writing
to ask you about your life and
how you cope with your fans//also
How many charities you support.?
But first I would like to ask
you how is are you and all of
your family// I know you are
very busy with things to
sort out and lots of important
things// I would relly like
to know how you cope with
so many fans I am one of them
but I've never had a chance
to meet you on any occasion.//
what charities to you support?
I know you support alot but
is it do you support banados
to yours or Sargents.of any other kind. Age 11
Sincerly I relly hope to hear from you very
Much * S   c   S   Zu.

Figure 3.13 Zoe's letter to the Queen (Year 7)

Stories

When I compared the stories that the pupils had written in Years 6 and 7 there was little or no evidence of progression in terms of the language used, such as more sophisticated vocabulary or the structure of the stories. In Year 6 they were given planning sheets to help with the structure; writing stories under timed conditions was also important preparation for the end of Key Stage 2 tests. In Year 7 the stimulus was usually provided by another piece of fiction, e.g. a continuation of a story by Roald Dahl, or a modern version of *A Christmas Carol*.

Two examples are given here of stories written by James, the first 'Out of the dark' (Figure 3.14) was written in the spring term of Year 6, and 'A Modern Day Christmas Carol' (the first half is in Figure 3.15) was written towards the end of the autumn term of Year 7. Both have violent themes and events, but the Year 6 story is shorter and more tightly structured. The Year 7 story went through two drafts (with feedback from the teacher) and was word-processed at home. There is little difference in the language used, for example the connectives are similar, e.g. the use of 'suddenly' several times in each story. The main difference is in the length, and this may have been because James had more time to finish the story in Year 7. There is no evidence from these examples of continuity or progression, unless one considers the greater length of James's Year 7 story as indicative of progression.

Summary

These examples of four different genres demonstrate that explicit teaching of how to write in particular genres had taken place in Year 6 rather than in Year 7. There was little evidence of planned continuity or progression in the pupils' writing skills in Year 7; if anything, these examples provide evidence of regression. However, this generalisation has to be treated with caution, given the relatively small number of examples considered above.

How did the target pupils see the differences and similarities in writing as they moved from primary to secondary school? In the next two sections I will consider the perceptions of the pupils when writing about and discussing their experiences of writing in Years 6 and 7.

Contradictory stories

I asked the four target pupils to keep writing logs during the autumn term of Year 7, though not in Year 6, and the writing logs showed that

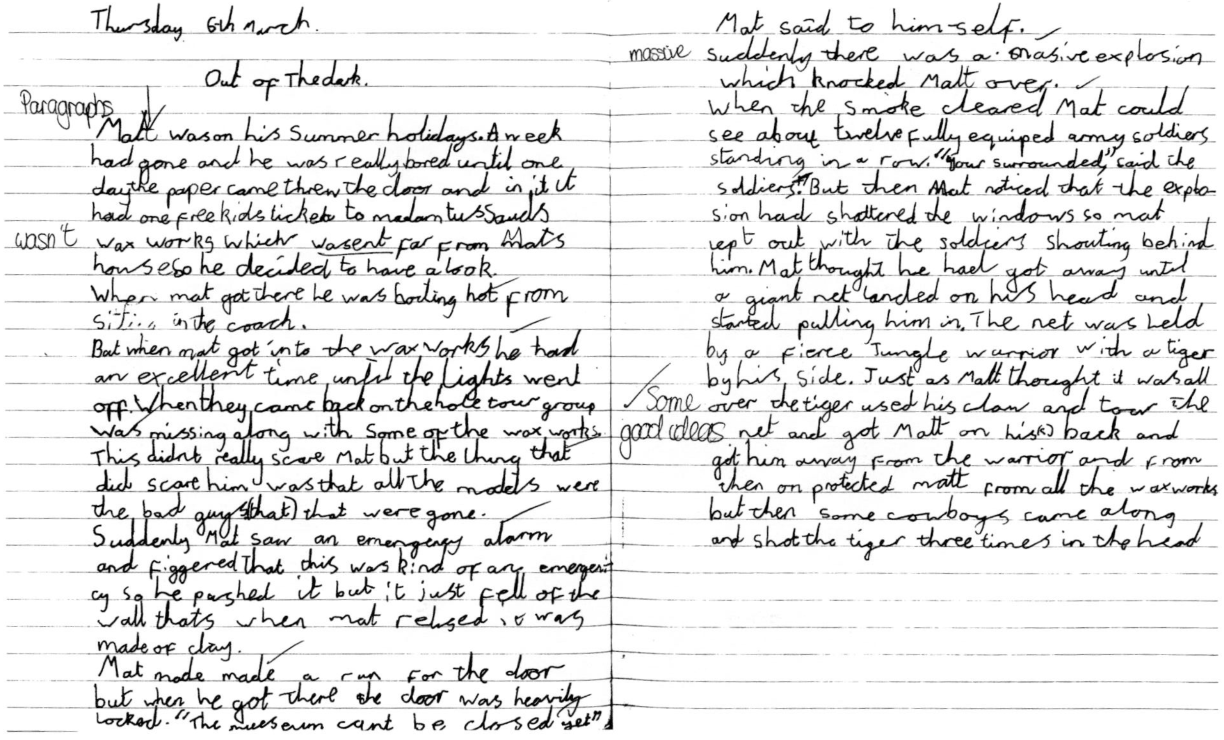

Thursday 6th March.

Out of the dark.

Paragraphs

Matt wasm his Summer holidays. A week had gone and he was really bored until one day the paper came through the door and in it it had one free kids ticket to madam tussauds wax works which wasent far from Matts house so he decided to have a look.

When Mat got there he was boiling hot from sitting in the coach.

But when Matt got into the wax works he had an excellent time until the lights went off. When they came back on the whole tour group was missing along with. Some of the wax works. This didnt really scare Matt but the thing that did scare him was that all the models were the bad guys that that were gone.

Suddenly Matt saw an emergency alarm and figered that this was kind of any emergency so he pushed it but it just fell off the wall thats when mat relised it was made of clay.

Mat made made a run for the door but when he got there the door was heavily locked. "The museum cant be closed yet!"

Mat said to himself.

Suddenly there was a massive explosion which knocked Matt over.

when the smoke cleared Mat could see about twelve fully equiped army soldiers standing in a row. "You surrounded" said the soldiers. But then Mat relised that the explosion had shattered the windows so mat lept out with the soldiers shooting behind him. Matt thought he had got away until a giant net landed on his head and started pulling him in. The net was held by a fierce jungle warrior with a tiger by his side. Just as Matt thought it was all over the tiger used his claw and tore the net and got Matt on his back and then ran away from the warrior and from there on protected matt from all the wax works but then some cowboys came along and shot the tiger three times in the head

✓ Some over good ideas

Figure 3.14 James's story 'Out of the dark' (Year 6)

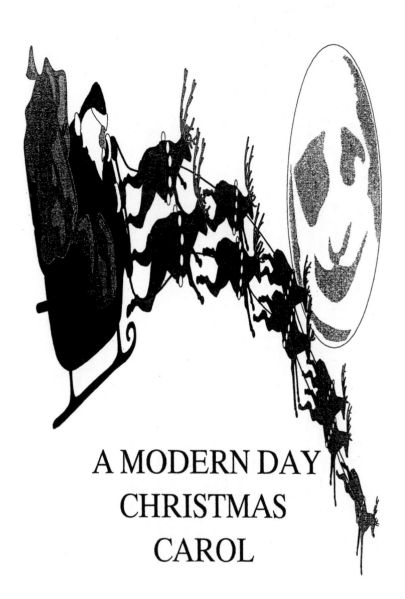

A MODERN DAY CHRISTMAS CAROL

It was an icy evening when Charlie went out in his car to the shops.
On the way he was caught in a traffic jam. Being the impatient man
that he was, Charlie tried to drive threw the gap that was between
the cars. When Charlie realised he could make it, he sped up to quite
a high speed, and then when he got more confident he started to take
his eyes of the road. Then just as he pulled a face at somebody while
passing, a police car drove out in front of him. Charlie did not see
him until it was to late. He smashed straight into the police car and
went toppling into the air and came down with an almighty smash.
Both people were injured but the policeman just managed to radio
out for an ambulance. Charlie was dying but nobody would help him
because they thought that he deserved it for being so stupid, so they
went to help the policeman. !(After about a month in hospital the *N P*
doctors declared Charlie physically fit, but what they did not know
was that he was not mentally fit. He decided that even though it was
his fault that he crashed, if nobody would help him, he would not
help anybody else.

A few days later when he turned up at work, he found that his boss
had died from a heart attack. This made it that Charlie became the
boss of the forever growing, channel 9-television company. Within a
year Charlie had made his first £1.000.000 and also been named the
nastiest person in the country.

One night when he was watching his £100.000 television,
There was a bang on the door; the problem was the cameras
Showed nobody in the building. Charlie pulled out his
Shotgun from the secret compartment underneath his desk
And loaded it up. Suddenly he door blew of its hinges and
Charlie's dead boss came crashing threw the door, out of fear, Charlie
shot his head of. The boss just picked his head back up and fitted it back
on his neck. He told Charlie that he had been so horrible that two ghosts
to try and improve his ways would visit him. If he did not improve his
ways he would be left to roam the spirit world never being able to have

peace when he died. Charlie was told that the first ghost would appear at half past seven the next night, with that the boss disappeared. So the next night came and Charlie even though he did not believe it, he started to get worried at twenty nine minutes past seven he started to get a bit worried, then half past came, yet nothing happened. At quarter to eight the door came flying open and a skateboarder came threw smashing things up. "Who the hell are you, I have just had that door fixed," said Charlie. I am the ghost of Christmas past and I have come to take you for a trip, would you believe it, into the past," repeated the skateboarder. "Wait a second, you were supposed to be here 15 minutes ago," shouted Charlie. "Sorry dude it was impossible trying to get here"anyway lets go, just stand on my board and we will be off. They got back to when Charlie was a boy; he was living in a very poor family asking his mum for the cheapest computer console there was. He thought that it was the only one that his mum might be able to afford, but his mum said no because she was going to treat the family by buying a turkey so they could not have any presents. "Enough enough just take me back home." Suddenly Charlie found him self in his chair as if he had dreamt it all, except there was still a bottle lying broken on the floor. The next morning Charlie woke up to find him on what looked like a giant cloud that was floating in the sky. Then Charlie noticed that there was a footballer standing next to him. "I am the ghost of Christmas future said the footballer, "I have come to show you what will happen if you do not change your ways. This is when you die, you are not greeved people just carry on with life, in a way their glad that your dead because they will not have any more hassle from you and they will be getting paid more with their new boss. To put it simply there is nobody that likes you. I will take you back now so you can improve". The footballer finally said. So when Charlie got back over a couple of years he became just like everyone else because all of the money that he made, he donated to the poor. Then when he did die he was laid to rest in the spirit world .

(A-)

BY

N/c level
A.

Target   set out speech properly –
new line for new speaker

Figure 3.15 James's story 'A Modern Day Christmas Carol' (Year 7)

(in terms of the pupils' perceptions) copying and answering questions were the writing activities that occurred most frequently. The Year 7 writing logs also showed how the children used different categories from me to conceptualise the writing they did in the classroom; hence the title of this section. The categories which I thought were significant, because of their relative high frequency in the pupils' exercise books, such as tables or charts, and labelling, were not mentioned, i.e. they did not count as writing for the pupils, and I had not mentioned these categories to them. According to the pupils' perceptions, much of the writing they did was largely repetitive and limited to a few types.

The pupils kept the writing logs for 13 weeks, and by the end of this period the entries were rather brief, and often consisted of a summary of the lesson. In my analysis I could only use entries which clearly described one or more writing activities. Here are two typical entries:

> French Today we did some copying up from textbook(s) into workbook.
> R.S. Today we answered questions off a worksheet into workbook.

These examples were evidence that, according to the pupil, copying and answering questions had occurred. Other entries summarised the lesson, e.g. 'finishing off'; or 'today we did a page from a textbook into our workbook', which could mean answering questions or copying or both. Entries such as these, which did not clearly identify the writing activity/activities, could not be included in the analysis of the writing logs.

In Table 3.4 the main categories from the writing logs in the two secondary snapshot weeks are presented. In the snapshot week beginning 22 September, references to copying and answering questions occurred most frequently, accounting for 61% of the types of writing identified. If the categories of test and worksheet are combined with answering questions (tests and worksheets usually involve answering questions), the proportion of these categories together was 70%. There were differences between the two boys; Gavin kept his writing log more conscientiously than James, and Lauren was more conscientious than Zoe. Comparison with Table 3.1 shows that while answering questions was identified as an important category in my analysis of the pupils' writing in the week beginning 22 September, and in the pupils' writing logs, the other most frequently occurring categories in the two sets of data were different, because they conceptualised writing tasks differently.

Table 3.4 Aggregated totals from the pupils' writing logs for the two secondary snapshot weeks

Type of writing	W/b 22 September	W/b 1 December
Answers	12	6
Cloze		1
Copying	22	7
Design poster/project cover	2	1
Explanation	1	
Final draft/neat copy	1	1
Label		1
Other	1	1
Personal writing	4	
Plan experiment		1
Poem	1	
Puzzle		1
Results/reports	3	5
Story		4
Survey	3	
Test	2	7
Wordsearch	1	
Worksheet	3	3
Totals	56	39

By the second secondary snapshot week (week beginning 1 December) the pupils were flagging, quite understandably, and the diary entries were much briefer than at the beginning of the term. The main categories they identified were copying, doing a test, answering questions, followed by recording results (in science) and writing a story (in English). If answering questions is combined with test and worksheet (totalling 42.1%), these categories plus copying account for 61% of the writing activities identified by the pupils. Comparison with my analysis of the pupils' writing in the week beginning 1 December shows a different picture (Table 3.1). Answering questions was the most frequently occurring category, and this was similar to the evidence of the pupils' writing logs (particularly if one combines answering questions with the test and worksheet categories), but the other frequently occurring categories were different in the two sets of data.

Interviews with pupils

The pupils were interviewed at the end of Year 6, and at five points in the autumn term of Year 7 (though not all the pupils were able to attend the interviews in Year 7). What were the similarities and differences in the pupils' perceptions of writing as they moved from primary to secondary school? The picture that emerges is a complex one, and the main categories I will use are:

- what types of writing the pupils enjoyed most or were pleased with;
- what they understood by 'good writing';
- the differences and similarities they experienced in writing in different subjects in Year 6 and Year 7;
- other issues raised in the interviews;
- how they perceived their progress in writing as they looked back from the end of the autumn term in Year 7 to the end of Year 6.

Enjoyment of writing

At the end of Year 6 Gavin, Lauren and Zoe said they had enjoyed producing their Victorian newspaper reports, while James had enjoyed writing stories. Six months later, in Year 7, James said that he still enjoyed writing stories (other writing was 'boring'), while Lauren liked writing poems; i.e. enjoyment was most closely identified with creative writing.

Good writing

At the end of Year 6 I asked the pupils what they understood by 'good' writing. All the children emphasised the importance of technical skills, such as neat handwriting and presentation, accurate spelling, and the correct use of punctuation marks. They said that they used dictionaries and thesauruses regularly to improve their writing. Gavin, James and Lauren said that they knew if they had produced a good piece of writing if the teacher wrote 'good' or 'excellent' in their books and gave them a star. When we discussed stories ('How would you know if your partner had written a good story?') Zoe said that a good story had to be interesting. Lauren mentioned 'detail and expression'; she also gave the example that in an information leaflet she would look for 'detail'. Gavin said a good story should be adventurous, mysterious and funny, and it should 'all fit together and make sense' like the Goosebumps story which he was reading. In the autumn term of Year 7 the pupils continued to emphasise the importance of neatness and technical accuracy as features of good writing, though they felt the teachers at secondary placed less emphasis on these features than their primary school teachers.

Material differences in writing at primary and secondary school

At the beginning of Year 7 the pupils were struck by material differences in writing, for example at the primary school the teacher would provide guidelines if the pupils had to write on plain paper; this didn't happen at secondary school. According to Lauren, she wrote stories in her exercise book and then on plain paper at primary school, and at secondary school she wrote her neat copy on A4 lined paper. At primary school pupils used pencil for drafting ideas, and there was much more emphasis on neat handwriting, using fountain pens or handwriting pens, while at secondary school they could use biros.

Editing and redrafting

The evidence of the interviews and classroom observation suggests that the pupils were (on the whole) making neat copies of corrected drafts in Years 6 and 7, though this was not always the case. For example, in Year 6 they emphasised the importance of planning ideas in their think books, which they discussed with a partner and/or the teacher. Their perception was that the teacher tended to say that their pieces could be longer, more detailed, or that their handwriting should be neater.

Editing and redrafting at secondary school were mentioned mainly in the context of English. For example, the pupils explained that the letters written in response to *Two Weeks with the Queen* (described above) were planned in exercise books, checked by the teacher, and written up neatly on A4 paper. Computers were sometimes used for editing and redrafting in English in Year 7, though this was not possible for the whole class in Year 6.

However, the fact that editing and redrafting usually meant correcting spelling and punctuation, and making a neat copy in both Years 6 and 7, could be interpreted as evidence of an unplanned similarity in classroom practice, but not of progression.

Copying

At the beginning of Year 7 I asked the pupils whether they thought they did more or less copying at secondary school, compared to the primary school. I received mixed messages in answer to this question. For example, Lauren said they had done more copying in Year 6. James agreed, and said that at secondary school they were given more encouragement to develop their own ideas. Later on in the interview they all agreed that they did a lot (or more) copying at secondary school than in Year 6. The pupils may have been trying to give me the answer they thought I wanted, though references to copying cropped up during the course of the term when the pupils described writing activities in different subjects. The evidence of the writing logs suggests that the pupils were aware of doing a lot of copying in Year 7, but I cannot conclude whether more or less copying occurred in Year 6 compared to Year 7.

Spelling

The pupils received mixed messages about the importance of spelling across the curriculum in Year 7, compared to their experiences in Year 6. In Year 6 the pupils regarded accurate spelling as an important aspect of good writing. They enjoyed regular spelling tests, and were competitive about them. In Year 7 they quickly became aware that attitudes to spelling varied across the curriculum. For example, in an interview conducted in September, they agreed that the subjects where spelling and punctuation were corrected most often were English, history, geography and religious studies. In English in Year 7 they used the 'look, say, cover, write, check' approach that the pupils were familiar with from Years 5 and 6. Their perception was that spelling was more important in some curriculum areas than others in Year 7, and they felt that this was a difference with primary school, where spelling was corrected more consistently.

The teaching of writing

I did not ask the pupils at the end of Year 6 how their teacher taught them to write in different genres, though I did early in Year 7. When I asked the pupils how they were taught to write different genres, their comments were mainly about the transmission and copying of instructions, answering questions, etc. In the first two months of Year 7 the pupils did not describe being taught to write a new genre or text type, and this is confirmed by the evidence of their exercise books. However, they were taught to write discursive essays later on in the year in history, as I describe in Chapter 4.

English

When asked about the main types of writing which they did in English during the autumn term of Year 7, the pupils referred to stories, letters, poems, book reviews and character studies, in addition to editing and redrafting on computers. They said that main differences in writing in English between Year 6 and Year 7 were that they wrote at greater length or included more detail, e.g. in book reviews or stories.

History

Comments about history at the beginning of Year 7 emphasised the similarities between Year 6 and Year 7. For example, Gavin said that the content of history was the same because it was about 'people in the past, Victorians, Greeks'. Later on in the term the pupils became more aware of differences in curriculum content, skills and responses required by their teachers in Year 7. For example, in October, James (taught in the same group as Gavin) described two activities in history that were new to him: a simulation of an archaeological dig in the computer room, where he had to write his findings in his exercise book; and learning about hierarchies. Pupils also took notes in history; this was something James had done in Year 6 (as I describe in Chapter 4), though the teachers did not know what strategies were used to encourage good note-taking in the 'other' phase.

Geography

James's comments about geography emphasised the differences in curriculum content and approach in Year 7, but not the teaching and uses of writing. For example, he described watching a video about open-cast mining in geography, and then writing about the advantages and disadvantages in his exercise book. Towards the end of the autumn term James described how he and Zoe had participated in a computer simulation, choosing the best place in school for a weather station, and then writing a 'short sentence' about their conclusions. This, too, was different from geography in Year 6.

In general, the pupils' perceptions were of a content-heavy curriculum in Year 7, with a greater variety of activities than in Year 6. However, they had little sense of progression between the end of Year 6 and the first few months of Year 7, in terms of learning to write in different genres.

Perceptions of progress

Towards the end of the autumn term of Year 7, I asked Lauren, James and Zoe if they had 'improved' as writers at the secondary school.

James was emphatic that he had not improved, though he felt he was doing more writing in Year 7, and Zoe also said she was now 'writing more'. Lauren felt she was writing more detail in her poems at secondary school, and her joined-up writing was neater. Thus, their understanding of improvement in writing included quantity, neatness and the amount of detail.

Concluding comments

The picture that emerges from this chapter is a complex one. It suggests a preponderance of chasms compared to bridges, i.e. a lack of planned continuity and progression in children's writing between Years 6 and 7. The evidence from the snapshot weeks showed that the dominant types of writing used at the end of Year 6 were different from those used at the beginning of Year 7. There was greater similarity between the types of writing used in the two snapshot weeks in the autumn term of Year 7. The teaching and learning of new concepts and ideas at the beginning of the secondary school tended to draw on the pupils' existing repertoire of writing skills.

Mixed messages were clearly sent to the pupils about writing by their different teachers in Year 7. The pupils' conceptualisations of writing, as reflected in their writing logs, showed that copying and answering questions were seen as the most frequently occurring writing activities in the autumn term of Year 7. This limited diet of writing activities is broadly similar to the findings of research conducted over 20 years ago. The extent to which this has changed since the introduction of the NLS will be considered in Chapter 6.

Implications for the practising teacher

The National Literacy Strategy in primary schools, and at Key Stage 3, has raised the awareness of some (possibly most) teachers about the need to teach writing more explicitly across the curriculum. If you have not already done so, you need to ask:

- What types of writing do I/we *need* to teach in Year 7, so that pupils can start to access the Key Stage 3 curriculum more effectively?
- When should these different types of writing be taught, using the most appropriate approaches from the NLS (e.g. studying the generic features of a text type; modelling the writing for the class; the use of writing frames, key words, starter sentences, etc.)?

- How can we combine the best features of our current practice with the explicit teaching of writing, rather that throwing out everything that was successful from our existing curriculum?
- How can we evaluate the success of our approach? For example, moderating samples of pupils' work in the department, observing one another teach, etc.?

This case study illustrates the importance of creating time for primary and secondary teachers to communicate about expectations and curriculum demands in Years 6 and 7, and this will not happen unless it is a whole-school priority.

4 Through the looking glass: the teaching and uses of writing in Year 6 and Year 7

Now here, you see, it takes all the running you can do, to keep in the same place. If you want to get somewhere else, you must run at least twice as fast as that!

Through the Looking Glass, Chapter 2.

Introduction

As I have outlined in Chapter 2, official documents and reports claim that there is clear evidence of regression for a significant number of pupils as they move to the secondary school. I wanted to gain a better understanding of what was 'going on' in this complex process of change and adjustment by investigating whether there were significant differences in the ways writing was taught and used in the classroom in Years 6 and 7. To investigate this dimension, I carried out classroom observation in both years.

This chapter tells a series of interlinked stories or mini-case studies about what I observed in the classroom, and what teachers and pupils said about the writing activities in these lessons. I hope that the chapter, though quite detailed, will also act like a mirror and enable the reader to reflect on what s/he does when teaching or using writing, and to consider how much current practice has improved in reality over the last four or five years. The NLS has made secondary teachers in particular think more about the pace and focus of their lessons. However, further research would be required to discover whether the teaching of writing has greatly changed the essentially conservative nature of classroom practice (cf. Medwell 1998). In this context the quotation from *Through the Looking Glass* could serve as an epigram (or possibly an epitaph) for all teachers who attempt 'to move things on' for their pupils in the face of an unending flow of initiatives.

Though I found evidence of a lack of planned continuity and progression between the phases, the differences in teaching and learning styles were less clear cut than I had anticipated. The most striking differences occurred between subjects in Year 7; this might have been predictable, but for a classroom teacher like myself it was an eye-opener. In telling the story of my period of lesson observation, I have tried to be sensitive to (what seemed at the time) the most important features of each lesson where writing was concerned.

I observed approximately 12 hours of lessons at the end of the summer term of Year 6 at the Fairway Junior School, and 13 one-hour lessons at the Joseph Priestley School in the following autumn and spring terms of Year 7. I did not observe the same genres being taught in Year 6 and 7, but I have described the techniques that teachers used and the processes that pupils experienced in the classroom. The notion of teachers' techniques can be divided into three main areas or subheadings, which I will use where appropriate:

1. The teaching of a particular genre, where I analyse the approaches that were used in terms of (for example) the teacher's explanation, uses of modelling and writing frames, etc. I consider how the purpose of the writing was linked to the teacher's learning objectives.
2. How the teacher taught a particular skill, for example, editing and redrafting, or note-taking.
3. Other ways that writing was used in the context of teaching. The main uses I observed were giving instruction, providing definitions or new pieces of information, and writing questions which the pupils answered (and sometimes copied as well).

Where appropriate I have combined the descriptions of what the teachers were doing with the pupils' responses and comments on the lessons.

The teaching of genre at the primary school

At the Fairway Junior School I observed the teaching of three fiction genres: scripts, newspaper front pages, and diaries. The main techniques used by the teacher were whole-class discussion, notes or guidelines on the blackboard for the pupils to copy, and discussion with individual pupils.

Writing a script

The teaching of script writing was part of a lesson on 'telejournalism', i.e. writing a TV news broadcast based on Penelope Lively's short story *A Flock of Gryphons*. After recapping the main events of the story, the teacher used these techniques:

a. he discussed different news programmes with the class;
b. he explained that they had to first write 'summaries' of the part of the story they were going to use;
c. he emphasised the importance of using 'interesting' vocabulary to hold the viewers' attention. He explained to the class how they could use the thesaurus to find suitable adjectives to describe the gryphons;
d. he pointed to the blackboard on which he had written a description of a gryphon, and two starter sentences for the pupils' reports.

This part of the 75-minute lesson took about five minutes. The pupils then spent 30 minutes working on their draft scripts, and the teacher circulated in the classroom, discussing the scripts with pupils individually and in pairs. In the last ten minutes of the lesson the teacher told the pupils to read through and revise their work.

From my observation of the pupils' exercise books, they tended to write their reports like a story or narrative. Gavin's report (Figure 4.1) was written as narrative, though it started appropriately 'This is Gavin Roberts reporting from London and I'm reporting to you about these peculior (sic) gryphons. . .' and he used some of the words and phrases he mentioned in discussion with me during the lesson.

The tendency to write narrative can also be seen by comparing Lauren's script (Figure 4.2) with James's (Figure 4.3). Lauren started the script in the required manner, and understood that the broadcast should include an interview from the scene (conducted by her friend). The numbers in the script indicated the different people who would be speaking, but the script did not really develop. James's script was more sophisticated, and he included interviews with two people, and an additional report with extra information. The format of his interview was like a story, but it was fluently written, and it was one of the scripts chosen by the teacher to be read out in front of the class.

Later, I filmed many of the pupils reading their completed scripts. After the class had watched the video, the evaluation of the presentations enabled the teacher to discuss aspects of the scripts which could be improved, with individual pupils. This extract shows how the teacher discussed Gavin's script with him:

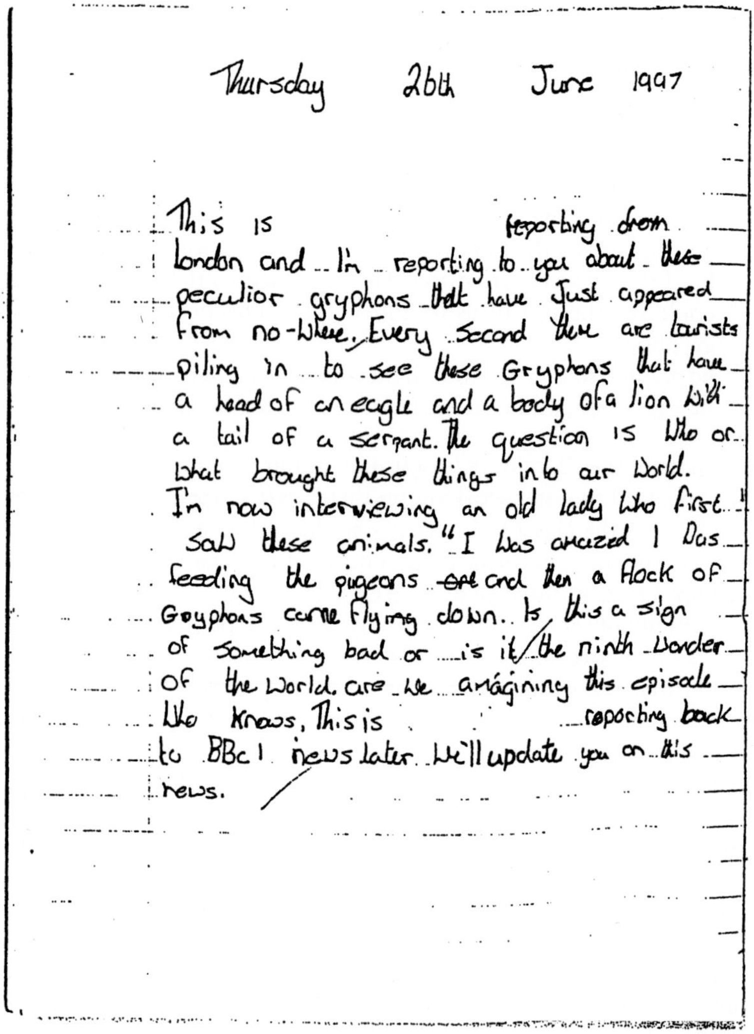

Thursday   26th   June   1997

This is   reporting from
London and I'm reporting to you about these
peculior gryphons that have Just appeared
from no-where. Every Second there are tourists
piling in to see these Gryphons that have
a head of an eagle and a body of a lion with
a tail of a serpant. The question is Who or
what brought these things into our World.
I'm now interviewing an old lady who first
saw these animals. "I was amazed I was
feeding the pigeons one and then a flock of
Gryphons came flying down. Is, this a sign
of something bad or is it/the ninth wonder
of the world. are we amagining this episode
Who knows, This is   reporting back
to BBc 1 news later. We'll update you on this
news.

Figure 4.1 Gavin's TV report about gryphons, from his 'think book' (Year 6)

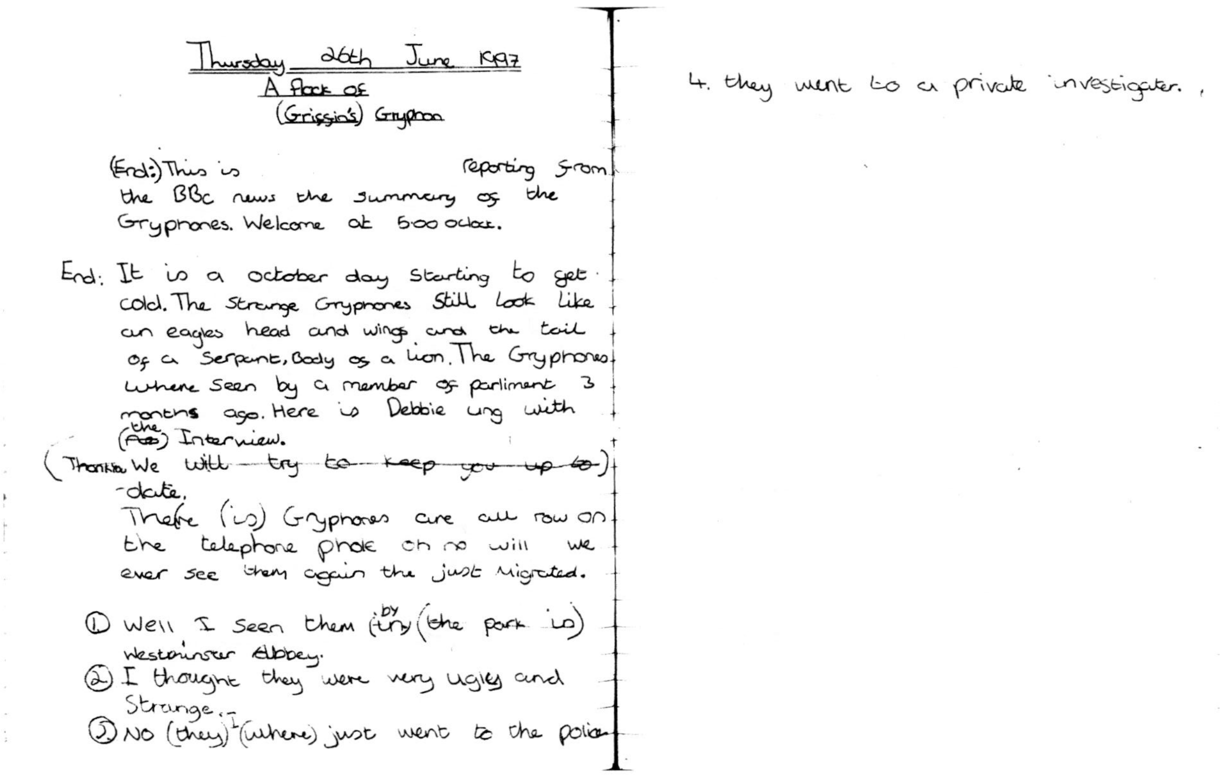

4. they went to a private investigater,

Thursday 26th June 1997
A Part of
(Grissini's) Gryphon

(Bob): This is _____ reporting from the BBC news the summary of the Gryphones. Welcome at 5oo oclock.

Ed. It is a october day starting to get cold. The strange Gryphones still look like an eagles head and wings and the tail of a serpent, body of a lion. The Gryphone where seen by a member of parliment 3 months ago. Here is Debbie with the ung
(Bob) Interview.
(Thanks. We will — try to keep you up to date.

Thanks. (Lo) Gryphones are now now on the telephone phone oh no will we ever see them again the just migrated.

1 well, I seen them (try (the park Lo)) Westminster Abbey,
2 I thought they were very ugley and strange.
3 No (they) (where) just went to the police

Figure 4.2 Lauren's TV report, from her 'think book' (Year 6)

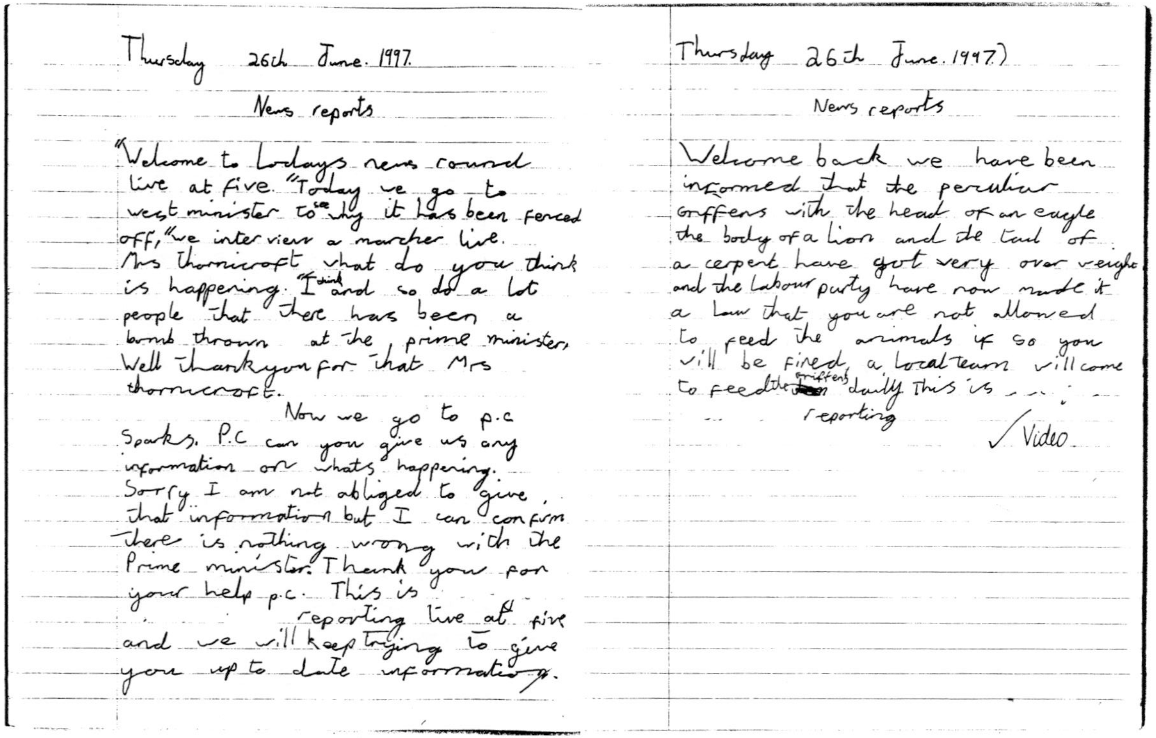

Figure 4.3 James's TV report, from his 'think book' (Year 6)

TEACHER: . . . you could have included more detail I think, a wide range of words do you think, words could have been included to make it more interesting for the reader . . . 'Every second there are tourists piling in to see the gryphons' . . . yeah, that's a good sentence. . . 'Every second there are hundreds and hundreds of tourists', that would sound better wouldn't it? . . . could you have interviewed someone else? What about the zoologist? . . . Look at the detail; you need a couple of sentences to say what is going to happen next.

The teacher continued to discuss scripts with individual pupils, and with at least six he commented on the need for 'more detail' and a more distinct sense of audience. Some pupils were told that they would have to rewrite the scripts, and possibly present them again. Figure 4.4 shows Zoe's script, and her subsequent evaluation.

Newspaper front page

This was part of the pupils' topic work on the Victorians. Work on writing contemporary newspaper front pages had occurred earlier in the year, and examples were on display in the classroom. In one 60-minute lesson the pupils were given a selection of topic books on the Victorians, and told to make notes on a topic of their choice that they were going to present as a front page of a Victorian newspaper. The teacher provided a worksheet that described the stages the pupils had to work through.

Most pupils worked in pairs, and the teacher circulated around the class. In the last ten minutes of the lesson the teacher discussed the use of headlines with the class, and elicited examples of headlines using alliteration from the pupils.

The focus of the 25-minute follow-up lesson I observed was the production of the neat or final copies of the Victorian front page in the pupils' project folders. The pupils were working from their notes, and draft pages in some cases, which they had made in the previous lesson. The main teaching strategies the teacher used were:

a. circulating in the class and discussing front pages with individual pupils;
b. telling the whole class to write in the present tense, and to include other features of a newspaper front page, such as headlines and the use of columns. He pointed to examples of pupils' newspapers about contemporary events that were on display in the classroom.

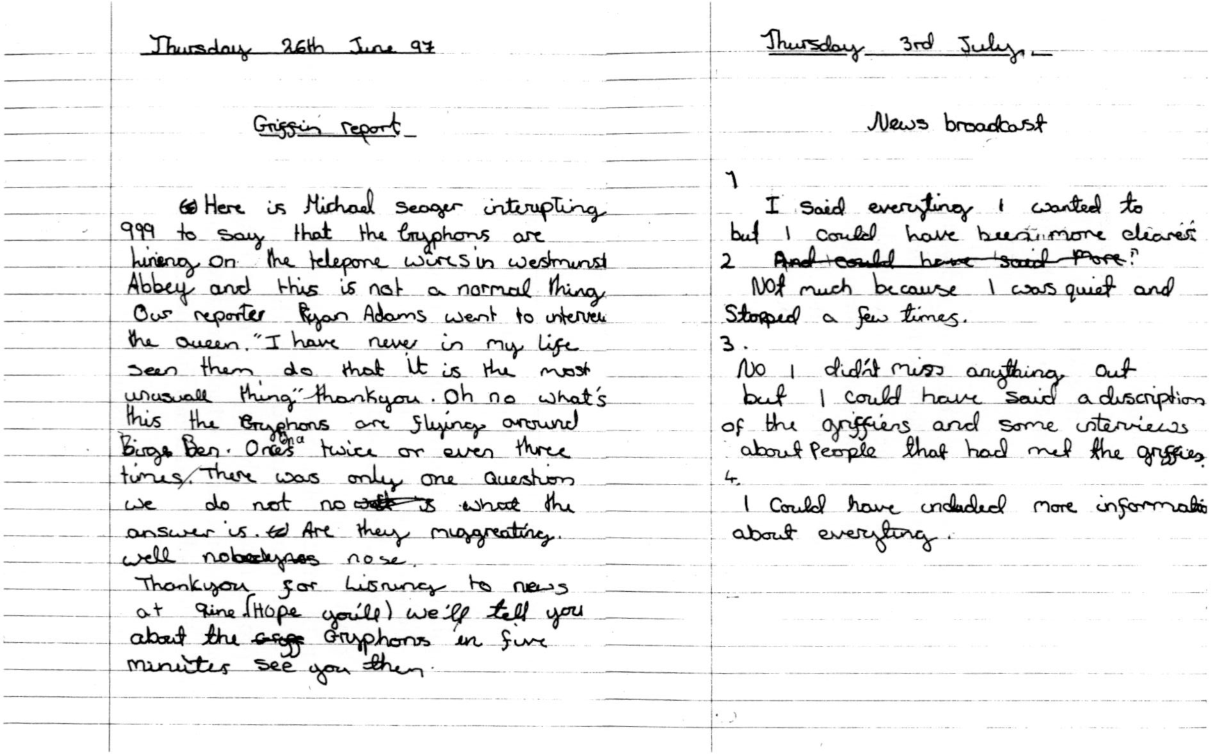

Thursday 26th June 97

Griffin Report

66 Here is Michael Seager interupting
999 to say that the Gryphons are
hiding on the telephone wires in westminst
Abbey and this is not a normal thing.
Our reporter Ryan Adams went to interview
the Queen. "I have never in my life
seen than do that It is the most
unusuall thing." thankyou. Oh no what's
this the Gryphons are flying around
Big Ben. Oh no twice or even three
times, there was only one Question
we do not no what is what the
answer is. to Are they suggesting.
well nobodyyes nose.
Thankyou for lisnuing to news
at five (Hope you'll) we'll tell you
about the Gryphons in five
minutes see you then

Thursday 3rd July

News broadcast

1
I said everything I wanted to
but I could have bun more cleaver
2 And could have said Port."
Not much because I was quiet and
stopped a few times.

3.
No I didn't miss anything out
but I could have said a description
of the gryffens and some interviews
about people that had met the gryffens.

4.
I could have included more informatio
about everything.

Figure 4.4 Zoe's TV report and evaluation, from her 'think book' (Year 6)

James's 'think book' shows the different stages he went through to produce the front page. At the first stage he made notes about life in the British Army, and his notes show that he was most interested in the improvement in guns and the invention of the machine gun (Figure 4.5). In the second stage, which took two lessons, James drafted a report which combined reports of a battle with information about the invention of the machine gun (Figure 4.6). The headline was somewhat cryptic 'In the Army you could lose your Armie (sic)', but the second page of the draft report shows how he was trying to describe the battle as if it was a recent event, reported by an eye witness. The style in part reads like his 'Telejournalism' report about the gryphons, writing as if an unspecified battle has just happened: 'We interviewed corpral (sic) Jones who helps powder the gun about what he thought of it . . .' The third stage involved writing the final version of his front page in his A3 project book. This had some of the formal features of newspaper layout mentioned above, and his report focused on the invention of the machine gun, and its effectiveness in battle (Figure 4.7). The tone was appropriately jingoistic for the period: 'But with the help of the machine gun the English Army made the foreigners drop like flies.' This typical example shows the processes that the pupils' work went through before the final version was produced.

Victorian diaries

The focus of this 35-minute lesson was writing a 'Victorian' diary, of the sort that might have been written by a child. When I came into the classroom, the teacher was talking to the class about Victorian times, and what it would have been like to be a child then. They spent about ten minutes discussing the sorts of things a Victorian child might have been concerned about, and on the blackboard the teacher had written:

> *Diary*
> Everyday happenings
> Things to be worried about
> Relationships with parents
> Hopes for the future

The teacher elaborated the guidelines that he had put on the board. The pupils were told to write entries for four or five days and to provide a 'Victorian' date. The aims of the lesson appeared to be:

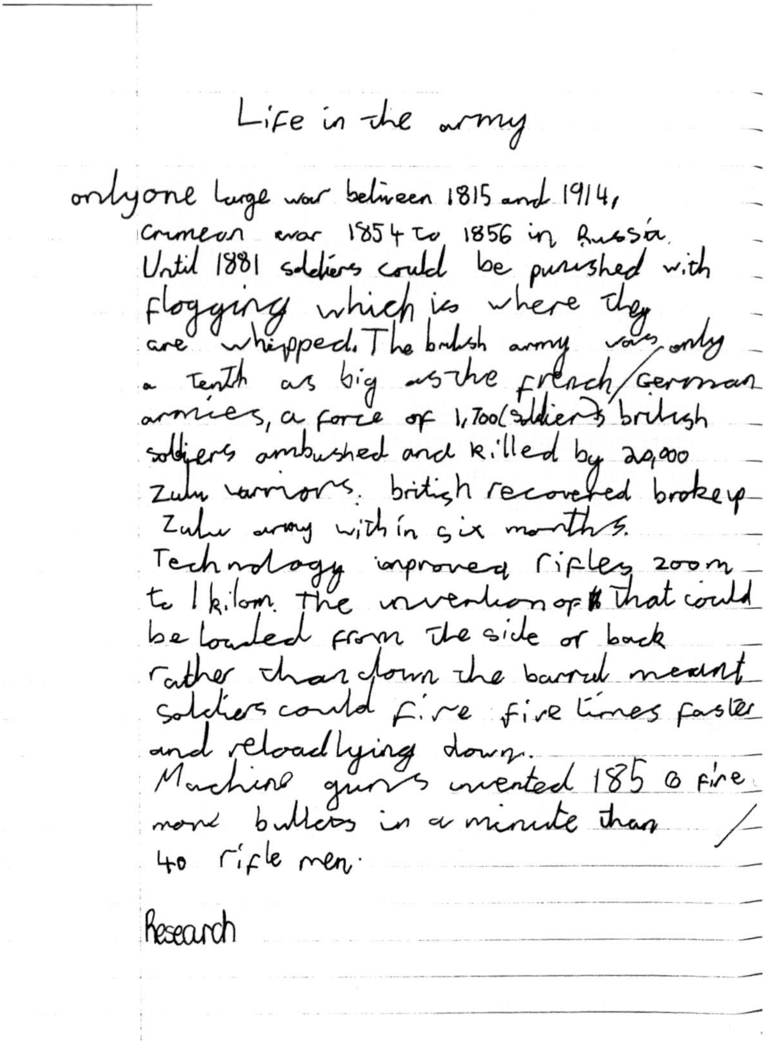

Life in the army

onlyone large war between 1815 and 1914,
Crimean war 1854 to 1856 in Russia.
Until 1881 soldiers could be punished with
flogging which is where they
are whipped. The british army was only
a tenth as big as the french/German
armies, a force of 1,700 soldiers british
soldiers ambushed and killed by 20,000
Zulu warriors. british recovered broke up
Zulu army within six months.
Technology improved rifles 200m
to 1 kilom. the invention of that could
be loaded from the side or back
rather than down the barrel meant
soldiers could fire five times faster
and reload lying down.
Machine guns invented 185 0 fire
more bullets in a minute than
40 rifle men.

Research

Figure 4.5 James's notes about life in the British Army, from his 'think book'
(Year 6)

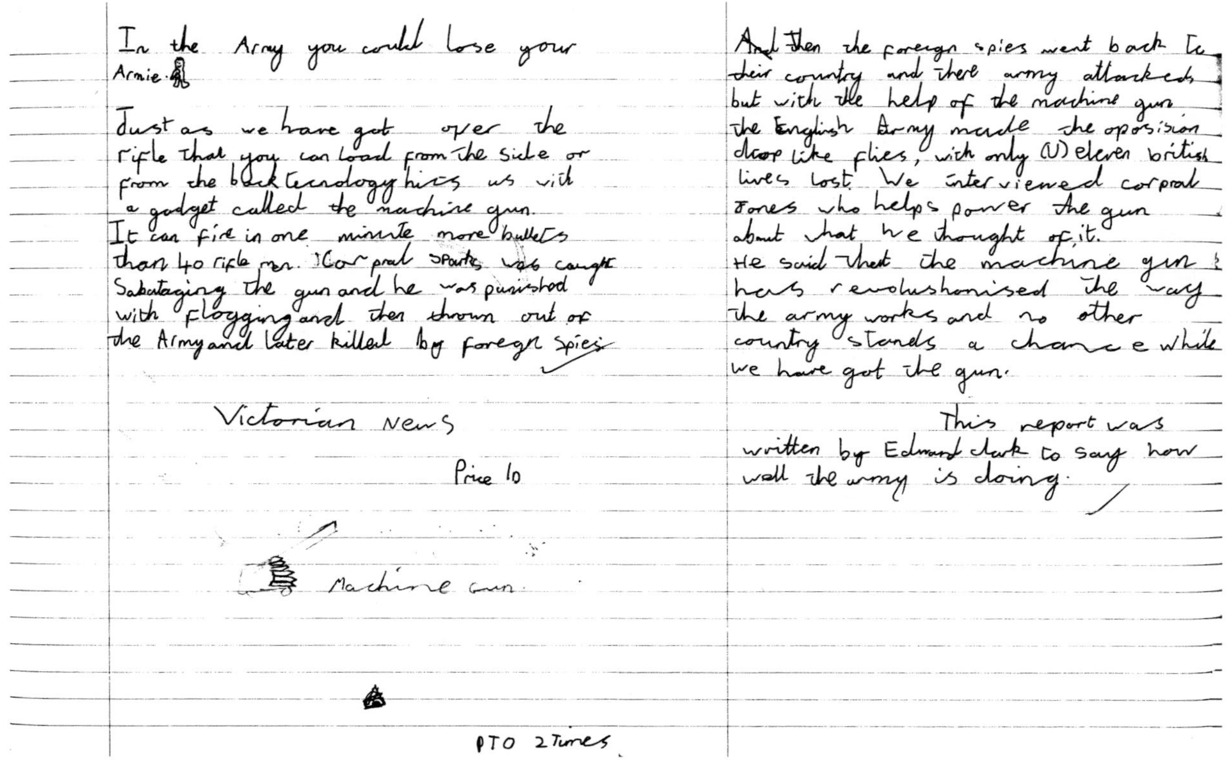

In the Army you could lose your Arnie.

Just as we have got over the rifle that you can load from the side or from the back Wendologg hits us with a gadget called the machine gun.
It can fire in one minute more bullets than 40 rifle per hour and Spouts. We caught Sabotaging the gun and he was punished with Flogging and then thrown out of the Army and later killed by foreign Spies.

Victorian News

Price 10

Machine Gun.

PTO 2 Times.

And then the foreign spies went back to their country and then army attacked but with the help of the machine gun the English Army made the opposition drop like flies, with only 11 eleven British lives lost. We interviewed corporal Jones who helps power the gun about what we thought of it.
He said that the machine gun's hers revolutionised the way the army works and no other country stands a chance while we have got the gun.

This report was written by Edmund Clark to say how well the army is doing.

Figure 4.6 James's draft report for his front page, from his 'think book' (Year 6)

VICTORIAN NEWS

Price 10
Date 1850

THE ARMYS NEW
INVENSION

Just as we 'have got over the rifle. That you can load from the side or from the back technology hits us with an invention called the machine gun. The machine can fire in one minute more bullets than 40 riflemen. Corporal sparks was caught sabataging the gun and he was punished with flogging then thrown out of the army and later

he was killed by foreign spies. Then the spies went back to there country and there army attacked. But with the help of the machine gun the English Army made the foreigners drop like flies. This report was written by Edward clarkTo show how well the army is doing

Figure 4.7 James's final front page, from his A3 'Victorian Project' booklet
(Year 6)

1. an exercise in empathy through writing a diary;
2. an opportunity to demonstrate what they knew about the life of a typical Victorian child.

Zoe's draft diary entry (Figure 4.8) shows that she had mastered some of the conventions of writing a fictional diary by using the first person. She combined a description of the opening of the Great Exhibition ('. . . I had just enough money to get in. . .') with an account of going to school.

These three examples (script, newspaper, diary) show how the teacher taught different text types using whole-class instruction, prompts on the board and work with individual pupils. The changes in approach in the same primary school, after several years of the NLS, will be discussed in Chapter 6.

The teaching of genre at the secondary school

I saw little direct teaching of genre during the lessons observed in Year 7, except in science and history. Where possible I will identify similarities or differences in the strategies teachers used to teach or use writing in Years 7, and those which I had observed in Year 6.

The science lesson: writing a report or recount

In the three Year 7 science classes I observed, the approach used for writing up the results of an experiment varied from teacher to teacher. In one science lesson the pupils were given a problem-solving activity, namely to find out how to dry a wet paper towel, and to see how long it took them to complete the task. In terms of reporting the results of the lesson the teacher's instructions were '. . . write it up, report how you did it. . . a nicely written report. . . underline headings, usual sort of thing'. In reality, his strategy was to ask the pupils to write 'about half a paragraph' describing what they had done in the lesson, and he did not insist on a formally structured report. The flexible approach was evident when the teacher told one child who had completed the task to 'do some writing as well. . . Or a couple of pictures to show what you have done, it doesn't matter'. Figure 4.9 is James's account of what he had done in the lesson, a short piece of personal writing typical of what most pupils produced in the lesson. In discussion with me during the lesson the teacher said that he spent the first two or three weeks of the autumn term teaching the pupils how to write reports, but he had a 'fairly relaxed' attitude towards it. Apart from two girls

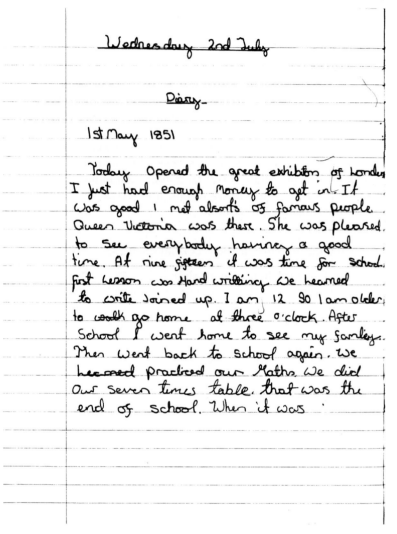

Figure 4.8 Zoe's draft diary by a 'Victorian' child, from her 'think book' (Year 6)

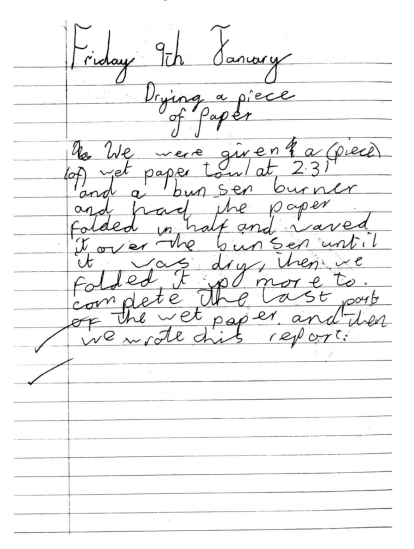

Friday 9th January

Drying a piece
of Paper

We were given a (piece)
(of) wet paper toul at 2.31
and a bunsen burner
and had the paper
folded in half and waved
it over the bunsen until
it was dry, then we
folded it up more to
complete the last part
of the wet paper. and then
we wrote this report.

Figure 4.9 James's account of drying a piece of paper in science (Year 7)

in the class who used a formal structure which they had learned in Year 5 to report what they had done, the rest of the pupils wrote a descriptive paragraph.

In another lesson pupils were learning about distillation, and the teacher started with a brief recap of the work of the previous lesson. The teacher's technique for helping the pupils to write a report was to put instructions for the experiment (distilling salt water), with headings for the written report, on the board for the pupils to copy. Before doing the experiment the pupils had to complete a worksheet on filtering, evaporation and distillation, filling in missing words to demonstrate their understanding.

There was no discussion in this lesson between pupils and teacher about how to write up the report. However, the heading and key words had been provided on the board. Zoe was the target pupil in the lesson, and I observed her working with a friend, completing the worksheet, copying the instructions, doing a diagram of the apparatus she used and labelling it (Figures 4.10 and 4.11).

The third science lesson I observed was also about the properties of water, and condensation and evaporation. There was considerable discussion with the teacher, for about 24 minutes of the hour lesson. The teacher wrote key terms and definitions on the board for pupils to copy into their exercise books. Seven minutes were spent with the class reading a section entitled 'Dry Up' in a textbook, about different states of water, and the nature of evaporation and saturation.

In the last 12 minutes of the lesson the teacher gave the pupils the 'wet paper towel' problem, and in groups or pairs they had to decide how they would dry the paper towel and what equipment they would need. In terms of writing the pupils wrote lists of equipment they would need on pieces of paper (along with a simple diagram of how the equipment would be used) which the teacher collected in. Some pupils added brief details of the methods they were going to use. For example, Lauren (the target pupil in this class) worked with two friends. They planned their approach in the back of Lauren's book; she did the writing and diagram, before giving it to the teacher.

At the end of the lesson the teacher elicited from some of the pupils how they would set out their report on this activity. The teacher asked what 'method' referred to:

IAN: What you do?
TEACHER: What else?
JANE: A conclusion.
TEACHER: What does that mean?

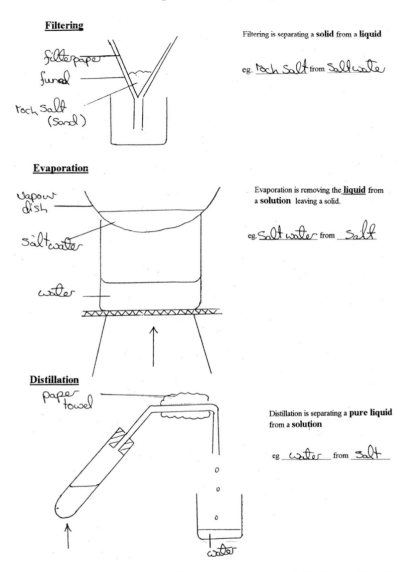

Filtering

filter paper
funnel
rock Salt
(Sand)

Filtering is separating a **solid** from a **liquid**

eg. rock Salt from Salt water

Evaporation

vapour
dish
Salt water
water

Evaporation is removing the **liquid** from
a **solution** leaving a solid.

eg. Salt water from Salt

Distillation

paper
towel

Distillation is separating a **pure liquid**
from a **solution**

eg water from Salt

water

Figure 4.10 Zoe's worksheet on filtering, evaporation and distillation (Year 7)

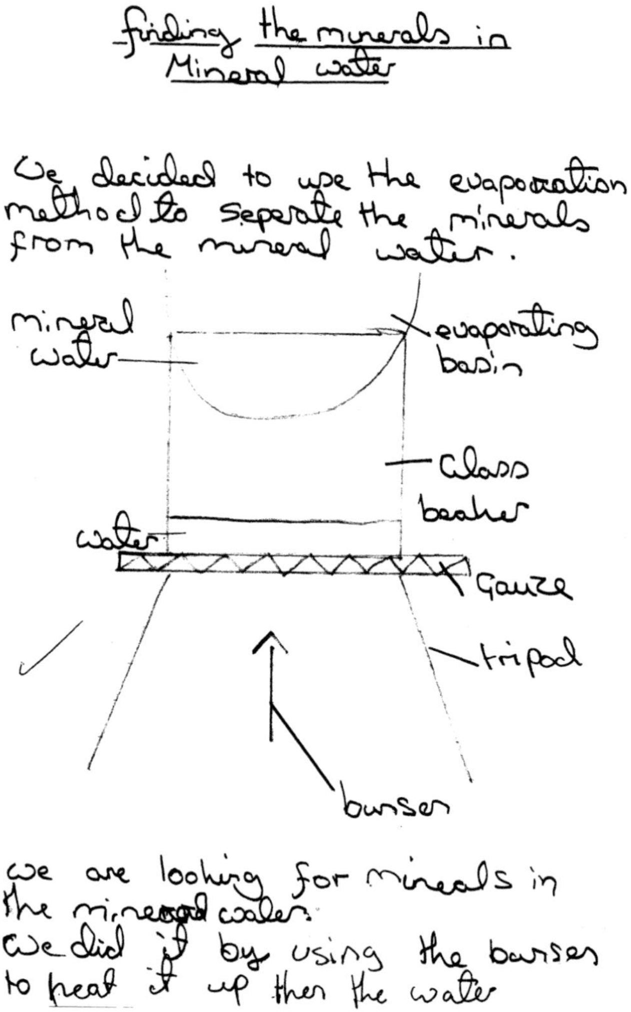

finding the minerals in
Mineral water

We decided to use the evaporation
method to seperate the minerals
from the mineral water.

mineral
water —

evaporating
basin

Glass
beaker

water —

Gauze

tripod

bunsen

We are looking for mineals in
the mineral water.
We did it by using the bunsen
to heat it up then the water

Figure 4.11 Zoe's description of the method she used to separate minerals from
mineral water (Year 7)

CARL: What you found out.
TEACHER: What comes in between?
PETER: The results.
TEACHER: What might your results be tomorrow?
PETER: How long it took?

We can see from this brief exchange that the students had some idea about structuring a report, and this emerged in the discussion with the teacher. Clearly, a variety of approaches was used by different science teachers in Year 7. In the lessons I observed, the writing of a formal report of the experiment was not insisted upon; it was more important that the pupils demonstrated their understanding of what they had done.

The history lesson: writing a discursive essay

I have included a detailed account of this history lesson, as it illustrates how the teacher taught Year 7 pupils to write a discursive essay about why the Normans won the Battle of Hastings. The main techniques the teacher used were:

1. To recap briefly the main events of the Battle of Hastings (each pupil had a summary sheet about the battle produced by the teacher);
2. To ask the pupils (in pairs) to sort out ten true/false cards about the Battle of Hastings into two piles;
3. Pupils had to copy the six true statements into the back of their exercise books, and work out why each of these statements helped the Normans to win;
4. The teacher described the beginning of the essay, and the need to start with a title and an introduction. The pupils had to draft the introduction in the back of their exercise books. The importance of the title, and the introduction, were explained to the class, so that the structure of the essay was clearly linked to its purpose:

TEACHER: Essays are questions, the title is 'Why did the Normans win the Battle of Hastings?' If you don't have that somewhere in your book, write it down now. The title does not say 'Tell Miss Bridges everything I can possibly find out about the Battle of Hastings', I'm not interested. All I want to know is why the Normans won, that is the title, make sure you've got it written down at the top of your page. . . OK. what's the next thing you write down?
KEITH: You write what you're writing about.

TEACHER: Right, you write something called an introduction, and in that, as Keith said, you say what you're going to write about . . . and your essay, of course, is about why the Normans won. What else is your introduction for? Alice?

ALICE: It's going to set the scene.

TEACHER: Right, good. It's going to set the scene. . . a bit of background information and says what your essay is about. . . what do you do once you've written your introduction?

HELEN: Write the paragraphs.

5. The teacher spent half the lesson (approximately 30 minutes) going through the six true statements, and discussing with the class why each statement made a difference to the outcome of the battle. The following extract was typical of the interactions that took place:

TEACHER: What was the advantage of the Normans being on a horse?

ALAN: Because you were higher then.

TEACHER: Right, we talked about this, didn't we? Being on a horse is a bit safer than being on the ground, it's much easier to fight down and much more difficult for someone on the ground to use their very heavy sword to stab up and kill you. . . What's the point of chain mail. . . ?

ALAN: Is it to stop the sword going through?

TEACHER: Right. So again it's to protect you from serious injury. So again you're less likely to die and less likely to get hurt. . . The Saxons didn't have any horses and very little chain mail, and more of them were likely to die. Less Normans were likely to die, therefore the Normans would eventually outnumber the Saxons. . .

6. The teacher explained that each 'true' statement would be the first sentence of a new paragraph. The teaching about writing the essay involved teaching the pupils how to write a paragraph. The teacher's approach was that a paragraph should be be structured in three parts for the essay, and she gave an example based on one of the statement cards:

TEACHER: Right, the first sentence – one reason why the Normans won the Battle of Hastings was they had more archers than the Saxons. This tells me what the paragraph's about. Then what you do is write a little bit about it, say perhaps about what the archers are and then explain why it was that having archers helped the Normans to win, OK? That's how you write paragraphs, that's basically what you've got in your books already . . . so six main paragraphs. . .

7. The teacher reminded the pupils of the need to start with an introduction ('to set the scene'), and to finish with a conclusion. In the conclusion they were told to pick out what they thought was the most important reason why the Normans won, with an explanation:

> TEACHER: Don't just say 'it was this reason', I want 'I think it was this reason because. . .', and tell me why you think that reason that you've picked is more important than the others. . .

Miss Bridges' aims had been to reinforce the approach to essay writing which the pupils had learned from their previous essay on the Roman army, and to get the students to explain and justify their reasons for the Normans winning the Battle of Hastings. The emphasis on an introduction, a series of linked paragraphs, and a conclusion provided the structure that the students could follow. As a result, most pupils enjoyed writing essays, and were successful at it.

Zoe's finished essay (Figure 4.12) shows that she still had to learn a number of different skills. The teacher's comments were supportive, and she identified what Zoe needed to do to improve: give explanations rather than a list of reasons, and structure her essay in paragraphs. The absence of capital letters for names was not commented on, except for 'Hastings' and two spelling mistakes. The explicit teaching of how to write a discursive essay in history was thus an example of unplanned progression from the writing pupils had done in Year 6.

The teaching or uses of writing skills in the Year 6 and Year 7 classrooms

The writing skills I shall describe in this section are: editing and redrafting; note taking; paragraphing; spelling and uses of key words; punctuation; recounts; answering questions; copying; labelling a diagram or figure; completing a table or a chart. Was there evidence of continuity and progression (planned or unplanned) in the ways pupils used these skills?

Why did the Normans
win the battle of
Hastings?

This essay is about the battle of
Hastings and why the normans won. it
includes when and were it took places.

all I introduction The battle of hastings took place on
a hill in 1066. The battle started in the
morning and went on all day. The Norman
had a strong leader called william Duke
of Normandy who never gave up. The Normans
had allsorts of wepons and armour they
had bow and arrows, swords, javlins and
chain mail which protects them. Halfway
through the battle gaps started appearing
in the Saxons sheild wall when some
saxons chased the normans down the hill
them they killed them. The normans tricked
the Saxons by pretending to retreat by
that time the men in the Saxon army
were either tired, carry injurries and dead.
So the reason why the Normans won
is because the Saxons got tired after
a while and were getting shot
by bow and arrow and there arms were
getting hit so they wouldn't be
able to fight and they would die.
The Saxons were more likely to die
because the Normans had lots of bow-
men so they could stand 10 metres
away and not get killed but the
Saxons had arrows coming wizzing
towards them and the Normans were

This is just a list of reasons, explain as you mention

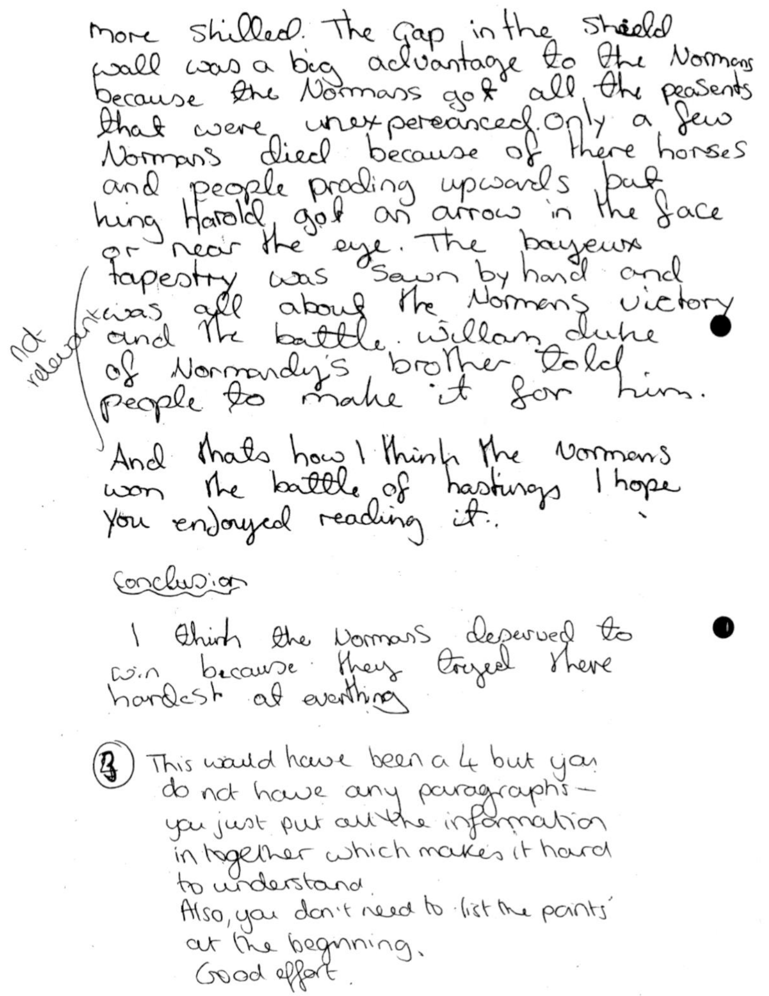
more skilled. The gap in the shield wall was a big advantage to the Normans because the Normans got all the peasents that were unexperearnced. Only a few Normans died because of there horses and people proding upwards but king Harold got an arrow in the face or near the eye. The bayeux tapestry was sewn by hand and was all about the Normans victory and the battle. willam duke of Normandy's brother told people to make it for him.

not relevant

And thats how I think the Normans won the battle of hastings I hope you enjoyed reading it.

Conclusion

I think the Normans deserved to win because they tryed there hardest at everthing

(3) This would have been a 4 but you do not have any paragraphs – you just put all the information in together which makes it hard to understand.
Also, you don't need to list the points at the beginning.
Good effort.

Figure 4.12 Zoe's essay about the Battle of Hastings (Year 7)

Editing and redrafting

Official reports (e.g. Suffolk LEA 1996) have commented that 'editing and redrafting' often means little more than making a neat copy of a corrected first draft, and this is what I observed (on the whole) in lessons in Years 6 and 7. In the primary school pupils made neat copies of drafts, for example of their Victorian newspapers, having corrected spelling and punctuation with the teacher's help. There was little direct instruction that I observed about improving the content of a first draft. For example, in the lesson on writing a TV news script ('telejournalism') the teacher told the pupils to read through their scripts and 'review' them:

TEACHER: I just want you to read it through . . . this is what you call the reviewing part, just read it through and see if you need to change any of it, add anything or take anything away. Just have a good read through, OK?

In the secondary school I observed Mrs Lee, working with two different classes in English, where the pupils were editing and redrafting their stories. In one lesson Mrs Lee was working with Lauren's tutor group on the stories which the pupils had drafted during the previous lesson. The teacher's expectations were that the pupils would write up their stories after editing and redrafting them. The stimulus for the story had been an extract from *George's Marvellous Medicine* by Roald Dahl, with questions, and the students had continued the story.

The teacher's strategy was to circulate around the class for about 35 minutes of the lesson, reading drafts and helping students individually. The focus (according to the teacher) was to help pupils improve the storyline, spelling, punctuation, grammar, use of describing words, and generally 'being able to express themselves'. The teacher's comments about pupils' drafts focused mainly on spelling and grammar, though with two or three pupils (girls) she commented approvingly on their choice of vocabulary. Dictionaries were available in the classroom, which were used by some pupils, though most of the spelling corrections were provided by the teacher.

In the second English lesson I observed, Mrs Lee was teaching her own tutor group (target pupils James and Gavin). The teacher's techniques were to spend five minutes recapping the task from the previous lesson, which was to write a modern version of *A Christmas Carol*, with examples from Dickens' story. Then Mrs Lee spent 20 minutes circulating round the class, looking at drafts in progress in exercise books, and corrected mistakes (mainly spelling, punctuation and the use of paragraphs), as well as making suggestions for improvements in the choice of vocabulary. Gavin's work on his story was typical of the processes that other pupils in class went through. Figure 4.13 is the initial brainstorm of ideas and list of characters that he wrote in his English exercise book. He drafted the story in his exercise book (Figure 4.14). Mrs Lee commented on the draft, and on the last two pages corrected a few mistakes in spelling and paragraphing. The final version of the story, written on A4 paper for assessment purposes, was similar to the first draft, though neater (Figure 4.15).

Gavin's story was influenced by the death of Princess Diana. It has a strong narrative line, and includes elements that relate to the British Royal Family, and a ghostly warning (derived from *A Christmas Carol*). There is not much descriptive detail or dialogue. As a result of the intervention of the ghost of his dead wife, Prince Jeremy changes his ways, and helps improve the world, while his two sons become kings, get married, and have children – there is a happy ending. The teacher's comments on this final version focused on spelling and the use of capital letters, and Gavin was praised for modelling his story on *A Christmas Carol*.

It would appear that 'reviewing' at primary school, and 'editing and redrafting' at secondary school were mainly about correcting spelling, punctuation and grammar, and making a neat copy. The teachers talked about the pupils having the opportunity to change their texts, but very little change of content took place. I did not see the teachers teaching the pupils how to improve the content of their work. Both Mr Taylor and Mrs Lee worked intensively with pupils on an individual basis. However, there appeared to be little or no difference in the process of editing and redrafting between Year 6 and Year 7; in both phases the pupils were making corrected, neat copies of their texts. Neither teacher knew what editing and redrafting involved at the 'other' phase; from these examples there was no evidence of either continuity or progression.

Note taking

I observed note taking in topic work or history lessons in Years 6 and 7. In the Year 6 lesson the pupils had to choose a topic on the Victorians that interested them from a selection of books, and make notes on it in their 'think books'. These notes were going to be used to produce their 'Victorian' newspapers. Note taking was not taught in the lesson I observed, but the teacher reminded the class of the need to pick out

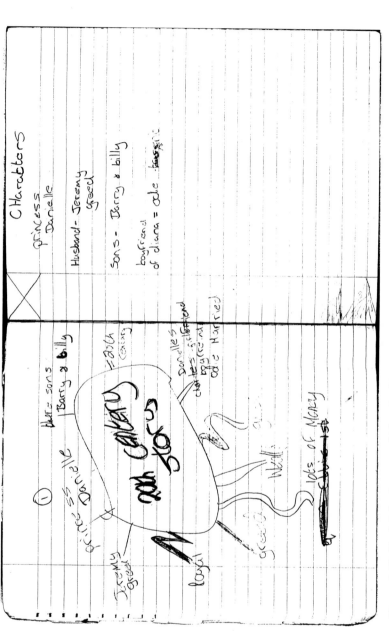

Figure 4.13 Gavin's brainstorm of ideas for his story (Year 7)

The Royal Success of the 20th Century

A Some of this story is based on the real drama story. In this story all names have been changed.

It all starts when Prince Jeremy is looking for a wife.

One fine summers day Prince Jeremy was playing with his royal golf team. Suddenly and all of a sudden Jeremy had a funny twitch and he looked around and noticed a beautiful-looking woman standing at the gates watching Jeremy play golf.

The first time they saw each other there was an attraction they saw looking at eachother for 5 minutes. Once he had snapped out of it he invited her in and from then on he cancelled most things

so he could spend time with Danielle.

As time went on Jeremy and their girlfriend Danielle got Married through the pregnancy, first came Prince Billy he caused little problems everyone rushing around.

By the time prince Billy was going to school prince Barry was born and he caused even more problems for them.

As the boys grew up Jeremy and Danielle gradually grew apart. As Jeremy started getting greedy about his money even more then he was before he not Danielle. Danielle found out that he was sick of Danielle and had a secret girlfriend. He They both decided to getting a divorce and Billy & Barry decided to go and live with their mother because they didnt seem to like their father anymore and were discussed when they found out about their father.

Figure 4.14 continued overleaf

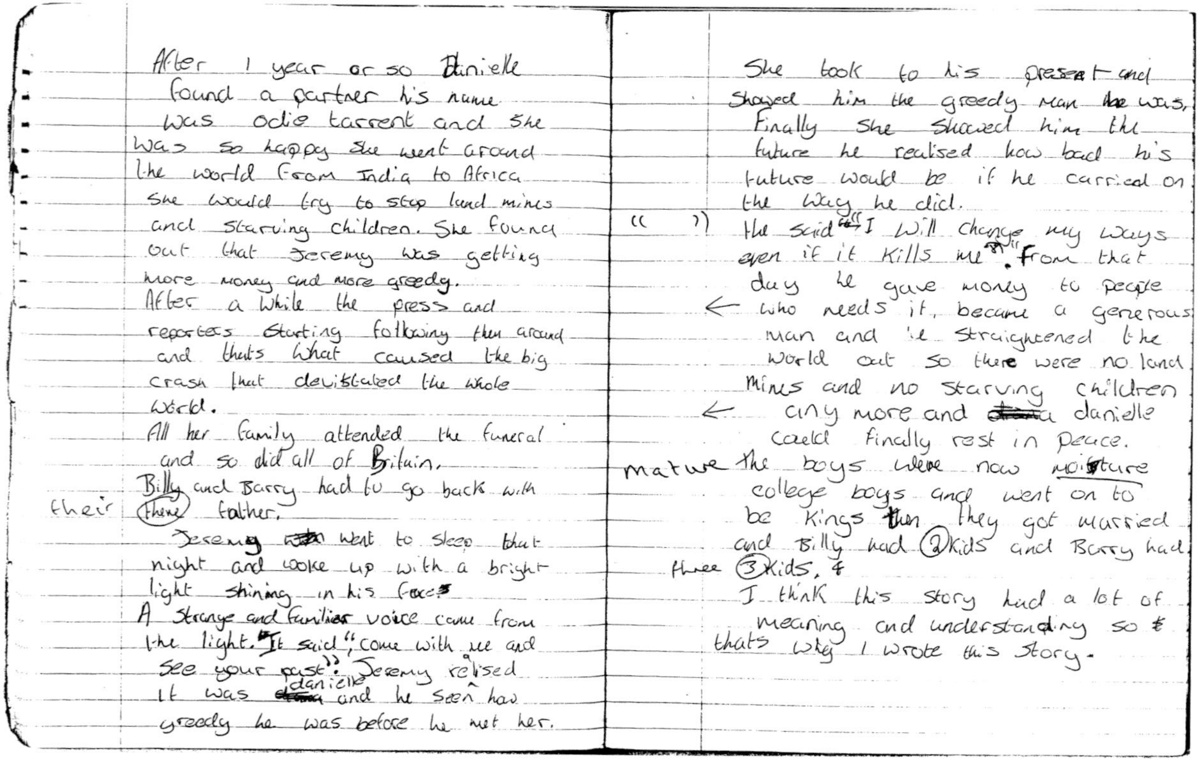

After 1 year or so Danielle
found a letter his name
was odie taccent and she
was so happy She went around
the world from India to Africa.
She would beg to stop land mines
and starving children. She found
out that Jeremy his getting
more money and more greedy.
After a while the press> and
reporters starting talking thu around
and thats what caused the big
crasa that devistated the whole
world.

All her family attended the funeral
and so did all of Britain.

Billy and Barry had to go back with
their father.

Jeremy went to sleep that
night and woke up with a bright
light shining in his faces

A strong and familiar voice come from
the light. It said "Come with me and
see your past" Jeremy raised
It was and he seen how
greedy he was before he met her.

She took to his present and
showed him the greedy man he was
Finally she showed him the
future he realised how bad his
future would be if he carried on
the way he did.

?) He said "I will change my ways
even if it kills me." from that
day he gave money to people
who needs it, became a generous
man and it straightened like
world out so there were no land
mines and no starving children
danielle

cry more and
caleb finally rest in peace.

mature the boys were now moisture
college boys and went on to
be Kings then they got married
and Billy had kids and Barry had
three kids.

I think this story had a lot of
meaning and understanding so t
thats why I wrote this story.

Figure 4.14 The first draft of Gavin's story (Year 7)

A Modern Christmas carol

It all starts when prince Jeremy is looking
for a wife.
One fine summers day prince Jeremy
was playing with his royal golf team.
suddenly Jeremy had a funny twitch and
he looked around and saw a beautiful looking
women standing at the gate watching him
play golf.
The first time they saw each other there
was an attraction, They were staring at each
other for five minutes, Once they snapped out of
it he invited her in and from then on he
cancelled most things so he could be with
Danielle.
   As time went on Danielle got married and then
got pregnant, Jeremy helped her through the
pregnancy.
First came prince Billy he (could) caused
very little problems with everyone rushing around
for him.
by the time prince Billy was going to school
prince Barry was born and he caused even
more problems for them.
As the boys grew up Jeremy and Danielle
gradually grew apart. Jeremy started getting
greedy about his money even more than he did
before he met Danielle.
Danielle found out that he was sick of her
and he had a secret girlfriend.
So they decided to get a divorce and Billy and
Barry decided to go and live with their mother
because they didn't seem to like their father any more.

watch capitals

Figure 4.15 The final draft of Gavin's story (Year 7)
      (continued overleaf)

sf

And were discusted when they found out about
sp there father,

After one year or so Daniele found a boyfriend
his name was odie tarrent and she was so
happy she went round the World from India to
Africa and she would try to stop land mines and
starving children. She found out that Jeremy was
getting more greedy.

After a while the press and reporters started
following them around and thats what caused the big
crash that devastated the whole world.

sp All her family attended the funeral and so did all of ●
Britain...

Billy and Barry had to go back with their father.
Jeremy went to sleep that night and woke up with
a bright light shining in his face.

A strange and familier voice came from the light.
It said "come with me and see your past" Jeremy relised
It was Danielle and he seen how greedy he was
before he met her.

She took him to the present and showed him
how greedy he is, Then he went to the future ●
and he realised how bad it would be if he carried
on the way he did.

The ghost said "change your ways". From that day
he gave money to people who needs them. He became
a generous man and he straightened the world out so
there were no land mines or no starving children
any more and Danielle could finally rest in
peace.

The boys were now mature college boys and went on
to be kings, then they got married and Billy had two kids
and Barry had three kids.

(B+) good vocabulary, you have followed Darren Robinson
the story through well. Target capitals !!

Figure 4.15 continued

'the important points'. Most of the pupils interviewed in the lessons explained note taking in similar terms, though for some this could also involve copying from the textbook.

In Mrs Dear's history class in Year 7, the pupils were doing group work on the Romans and preparing a display. At the beginning of the lesson she reminded the pupils that they had to read a paragraph from the book they were using, close the book, and write down the main points 'in their own words'. Of the eight students I interviewed in the lesson, seven claimed to be doing this. The ability to word process their notes at home was a motivating factor for some of the boys. There was not a striking difference in the approaches to note taking in history in Years 6 and 7, except that in Year 7 the pupils had to close the history textbook before writing their notes; this reflected the approach of the department.

I observed note taking in other Year 7 lessons. For example, in science pupils made their own short notes when planning an experiment (see above). In a mathematics lesson on polygons the teacher encouraged the pupils to jot down notes about what they already knew about polygons, though none of the pupils I observed did so. In these examples, note taking was used by pupils (or could have been used) to record their own ideas or knowledge.

Paragraphing

In the primary school the teacher assumed that his pupils knew how to write paragraphs, because they had already been taught to use them. However, on occasion he would remind the pupils of the importance of using paragraphs. In the secondary school paragraphing was referred to by Mrs Lee during an English lesson, while the pupils were editing and redrafting their stories based on *A Christmas Carol*. She reminded the class when to use paragraphs: 'change of time, place or a twist to the story, use a new paragraph'. The reminder was prompted by the fact that some pupils were not using paragraphs.

As we have already seen, the teaching of paragraphing was an integral part of Miss Bridges' approach to teaching the writing of argumentative essays in history. She taught that each paragraph consisted of three parts: the opening statement (e.g. the Normans won the Battle of Hastings because they were on horseback); a bit more detail; and the reason why this made a difference. This explicit teaching of paragraphing, linked to the structure of the essay, appeared to be an example of unplanned progression from Year 6.

Spelling

There were two approaches that I observed. First, the correcting of spelling in the pupils' work. This occurred in both primary and secondary classrooms, particularly in English and history lessons. Second, the introduction of a specialist or technical term, the meaning of which had to be explained and the spelling learned. I observed this in history, mathematics and science lessons in the secondary school.

In the primary school lessons, the correction of spelling was an important part of the teacher's interaction with pupils while they planned their work in their 'think books'. He would work with pupils individually during part of the lesson, correcting their spelling or asking pupils to look up a word in a dictionary. At the secondary school, similar approaches were also used in some Year 7 lessons. In the English class which Lauren belonged to, many pupils wrote new words or corrected spellings in their spelling books, using the 'Look, say, cover, write, check' method.

The two history teachers I observed provided the spelling of key historical words or names. In addition, Mrs Dear saw every pupil individually, checked the notes they had made in their exercise books, and corrected spelling mistakes, particularly of technical or complex words such as 'citizen', 'social occasion', 'socialise'. Misunderstandings were also corrected, for example the student who wrote 'pubic toilets' rather than 'public', and explained that the Romans didn't mind 'exposing themselves'. The teacher commented 'they didn't mind going in public would be better, wouldn't it?' Both teachers gave spelling tests to teach important historical words, and this was departmental policy.

The spelling of technical words was also important in mathematics, for example in a lesson on polygons, the teacher emphasised at least six times to the class the importance of copying the names of the different polygons correctly off the board into their exercise books.

In two of the science lessons, key words were written on the board, as part of the discussion with the class about the main concepts in the experiment they were going to do, for example 'dissolve' and 'evaporate'. This reinforced the teaching point of the lesson and showed the pupils how to spell the key words. A similar approach was used in modern foreign languages. For example, in a French lesson, the teacher wrote vocabulary on an OHP which the pupils needed to write two sentences describing their appearance, e.g. hair style, eye colour. Technical Vocabulary Checklists (lists of key words in each subject) were being introduced and displayed in classrooms around the secondary school.

Similar approaches to the correction of spelling mistakes in pupils' draft work in English and history were observed in both primary and secondary classrooms, but this cannot be regarded as evidence of either continuity or progression.

Punctuation

I did not observe teachers in Year 6 or Year 7 explicitly teaching punctuation, but teachers in both phases used similar approaches to correcting punctuation mistakes in pupils' written work, mainly by working with them individually at the planning or drafting stage.

Recount

I did not see pupils writing recounts in the Year 6 class, though there were examples in their exercise books. I observed the writing of recounts in secondary English, where pupils filled in self-assessment sheets about their progress during the term, and reading records, which included their views about the books they had read. In French, pupils wrote two sentences describing 'Mon Look', using vocabulary put on the board by the teacher. In science, some of the pupils wrote a recount describing what they had done in the lesson. It would appear that there was not much difference in the use of recounts between Years 6 and 7.

Answering questions

In lessons in both Years 6 and 7, pupils were observed writing answers to questions. For example, in the primary school pupils answered questions about poems; about the presentation of their TV script; and on worksheets in skills lessons.

In Year 7 lessons, pupils answered questions frequently, for example from a worksheet in science about distillation. In geography, pupils answered questions on the differences between two farms. In German, pupils finished incomplete sentences which had been written on the board, and filled in a grid with answers in response to a tape. Depending on the subject, answering questions was used widely in both phases. In the examples described above, answering questions was used mainly to test understanding and knowledge in both Years 6 and 7, though this is not evidence of either continuity or progression.

Copying

I observed pupils copying from the board, out of a textbook or from a worksheet in Years 6 and 7, though more frequently in Year 7. In the Year 6 lessons, pupils copied the definition of what a gryphon was and the opening lines for their TV scripts from the board. In design and technology, and in the lesson on poetry, pupils copied questions from a worksheet into their exercise books before answering them.

In the Year 7 lessons copying usually consisted of copying instructions, definitions or key terms, and I observed this in mathematics, science and history. In history, pupils also copied six true statements about the Battle of Hastings from the ten true/false cards, as preparation for writing a discursive essay. In geography pupils copied the title of the activity from the board and in German pupils copied incomplete sentences which they had to finish in their exercise books. These examples show the range of learning contexts in which copying took place in Years 6 and 7, though they are not evidence of either continuity or progression.

Labelling a diagram or figure

I did not see pupils labelling a figure or a diagram in primary lessons, though there were examples in their exercise books. In the secondary school labelling a figure or a diagram was observed in four different subjects. In the mathematics lesson about polygons, pupils copied the teacher's drawings of polygons and labels off the board and discussed them in pairs. In the science lesson on the distillation of salt water, the pupils drew a diagram of the apparatus used and labelled it, to show their understanding of how to set up the experiment. In geography, the pupils were given a photocopied sketch of two different farms and in pairs they had to label important features, using technical terms supplied on a worksheet. This activity tested their understanding of the terms, for example 'rough grazing'. The teacher circulated round the class checking whether the labels were put in the correct places. In French pupils drew and labelled a face from the description given orally by the teacher. This activity tested the pupils' listening skills and their understanding of vocabulary which they should have learned for homework.

These examples show that one of the main use of labelling observed in Year 7 was to give pupils opportunities to present information or ideas in different forms, thereby consolidating and/or testing their understanding, and this was broadly similar to the use of labelling in the pupils' exercise books in Year 6.

Completing a table or a chart

I did not observe pupils completing a chart or table during lessons in Year 6, though there were examples of completed charts or tables in their exercise books. In a Year 7 mathematics lesson, pupils copied a chart about lines of symmetry out of the textbook and completed it. This activity was intended to reinforce and test their understanding. In a German lesson the pupils copied a grid or table from the board and filled in the correct answers in the appropriate boxes or sections, in response to questions on a tape. This activity enabled the teacher to assess the pupils' understanding and listening skills.

Comment

I saw the pupils do a lot of writing in both phases, but teaching pupils how to write in a particular genre occurred infrequently. In Year 7 lessons teachers tended to draw on the repertoire of skills which they assumed the pupils had acquired in Year 6. Many of the uses of writing by teachers, and the writing activities experienced by pupils, were broadly similar in Years 6 and 7; there was no evidence of planned continuity or progression. Teaching pupils how to write a discursive essay in history in Year 7 was the only example of unplanned continuity and progression in the teaching of writing, compared to Year 6, that I observed. In the majority of cases, the Year 7 teachers were introducing pupils to new concepts, ideas and skills in the Key Stage 3 curriculum, but they were not explicitly developing their writing skills. Since I conducted my case study, the NLS has provided primary and secondary teachers with a shared language for the teaching of writing. I will consider the effects of this on continuity and progression at the primary–secondary interface in Chapter 8.

Implications for the practising teacher

This chapter raises questions about the types of writing that pupils do (typically) in Years 6 and 7.

- You could ask a small group of pupils to take part in a small research project, and review with them the types of writing they were asked to do across the curriculum in a week. Was there a variety of writing tasks, or was there a limited 'diet'? For example, was there a disproportionate amount of copying (you would need to ask the pupils to highlight what had been copied), answering questions, making notes and writing recounts? This is clearly a question that still needs to be asked, particularly if claims are made for the impact of the NLS on teaching and learning. What are the implications of your findings for teaching and learning, and for continuity and progression with the 'other' phase?

- What approaches are used, in reality, to teach writing in your school? Most teachers have had some training in the techniques recommended in the NLS for the teaching of writing. Are these being used consistently in your department? Teachers in a department, or across departments, could observe each other teaching, and (for example) learn from a colleague who has expertise in teaching a specific genre, but time needs to be made available for this, and for discussion afterwards.

- At a practical level, the Literacy Co-ordinator could play a crucial role in monitoring the teaching of writing across the curriculum, and helping colleagues learn from each other's good practice. Ideally, this should not only happen within a school, but between primary and secondary schools. Yet again, the identification of whole-school priorities, and the lack of time, are the main issues.

5 Can you walk a little faster? Secondary school teachers' views of writing

'Can you walk a little faster?' said a whiting to a snail,
'There's a porpoise close behind us, and he's treading on my tail.
See how eagerly the lobsters and the turtles all advance!
They are waiting on the shingle – will you come and join the dance?
Will you, won't you, will you, won't you, will you join the dance?
Will you, won't you, will you, won't you, won't you join the dance?'
Alice's Adventures in Wonderland, Chapter 10.

Introduction

Teachers are used to being told to do more, or to do it in less time, and to do it better, particularly where the raising of standards is concerned. Unlike the whiting or the snail we can't choose whether or not to join this particular dance. The unbelievable (and probably unsustainable) rise in Key Stage 2 results has created an irresistible pressure at Key Stage 3. We all want to raise standards, even if in practice this means teaching to the test, and using a range of strategies to achieve this goal.

I would like to think that we are neither whitings nor snails, but oysters, containing our unique pearls of knowledge created through learning on the job. The oysters, it will be remembered, rushed forward with the best of intentions for their walk along the beach, but they were duped, and eaten up by the Walrus and the Carpenter. I don't want to stretch the analogy, least of all in a way that trivialises the concerns of this book. However, teachers have had little or no choice about implementing the NLS; their existing knowledge and skills often appear to be undervalued by the policy makers as a result.

In this chapter and Chapter 6, I come to the third dimension of my research: an analysis of what secondary teachers think about the teaching and uses of writing in Year 7, including teachers' views about the effects of government policy. This chapter is based on the situation in 1997/98 when I did the original case study, before the introduction of the National Literacy Strategy at Key Stage 3. At that time, I conducted interviews with five Heads of Department at Jeremy Priestley School, and carried out a survey at both secondary schools in Billesley. There were over 100 teachers at the two schools, and I received 59 returns, of which 37 were from Jeremy Priestley School. Chapter 6 consists of interviews conducted in 2002 with the same teachers, or with teachers who replaced them if the original members of staff had changed jobs. I shall describe how the teachers involved thought the teaching and uses of writing had changed as a result of the NLS, and I hope that this perspective will enable us to see more clearly where the underlying problems of continuity and progression have persisted, and to identify areas where there have been positive as well as negative effects.

I did not conduct a survey with the primary teachers of Year 6 in Billesley so I cannot make cross-phase comparisons. However, I did interview Mr Taylor, the Year 6 teacher in the Fairway Junior School, about his approaches to the teaching of writing, and his expectations of writing in Year 7. By 2002 he had left the school, so I interviewed two of his colleagues who taught Year 6 classes; I discuss these interviews in Chapter 6.

In this chapter I focus on three main aspects of teaching writing that emerged from the survey:

1. Teachers' expectations and ideals about writing in Year 7.
2. The types of writing that pupils did in Year 7 lessons, and the sorts of writing mistakes that teachers corrected.
3. The techniques and approaches teachers used to teach different types of writing and writing skills.

The interviews had a broader focus and included other questions, such as the importance and effects of the end-of-key stage tests on approaches to writing, what the teachers understood by the term 'standard English', and the effect of the teachers' own educational experiences on their views about writing.

Teachers' expectations and ideals about writing in Year 7

Teachers' views on their role as teachers of English

Out of 59 teachers, 43 (i.e. approximately 70%) said they had a role as a teacher of English, which indicated a positive attitude to whole-school literacy several years before the introduction of the National Literacy Strategy at Key Stage 3. The comments written by some respondents indicated the importance of teaching pupils to write in complete sentences, and to spell correctly. Typically, one ADT teacher commented, 'Really, this is everybody's job, but I don't *teach* it – I merely correct it (i.e. mistakes in punctuation and spelling).' Comments from other teachers reflected priorities in different subjects. For example, a mathematics teacher wrote that he taught 'mainly short, precise answers in words/sentences or numbers', and a science teacher identified the need to teach 'logical progression, clarity of expression', while a geography teacher taught 'writing answers in full sentences with reasoning'.

The writing skills that teachers expected new pupils to have at the beginning of Year 7

Most of the teachers who replied to the survey identified their expectations about writing with basic skills. Thus the majority of teachers expected new pupils to be able to use capital letters correctly, write in sentences, use full stops, copy accurately, produce neat copies of their work, answer questions and know how to use a dictionary. Under half the teachers expected new pupils to be able to produce first drafts, write in paragraphs, or write stories.

The data from different subject areas reflect different priorities. For example, the four highest totals for the expectations of English teachers were: writing stories, writing sentences, producing a neat copy of your work, and the correct use of capital letters (Figure 5.1). This reflects the emphasis given to the writing of narrative at secondary school, though only three out of eleven English teachers expected new pupils to be able to write in paragraphs.

The main expectations of humanities teachers were that new pupils would be able to use full stops, copy accurately, use capital letters, use a dictionary, answer questions, and write in sentences (Figure 5.1). Teachers of mathematics and science had similar expectations, which reflected the short writing tasks, such as answering questions, which pupils did at the beginning of Year 7.

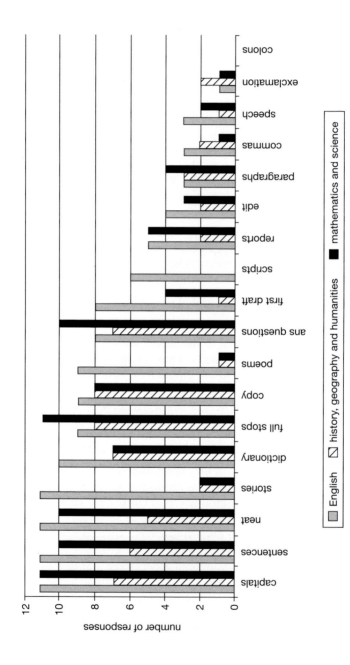

Figure 5.1 Writing skills expected of new pupils in Year 7 (by subject)

Legend:
- English
- history, geography and humanities
- mathematics and science

Y-axis: number of responses (0, 2, 4, 6, 8, 10, 12)

X-axis categories: capitals, sentences, neat, stories, dictionary, full stops, copy, poems, ans questions, first draft, scripts, reports, edit, paragraphs, commas, speech, exclamation, colons

The perception that presentational skills were emphasised at primary school, and that many primary pupils lacked adequate grammatical knowledge, was evident in responses from about 20% of the teachers. Typical comments included:

> Science teacher: 'Variable quality – most very competent, some of almost unreadable standard'.
> History teacher: 'Generally poor. Misunderstanding of use of capital letters, full stops, etc. *Many* students do not write coherently.'
> French teacher: 'They have no clue about English grammar, which I find incredible. I need to teach English grammar to them so they understand French better!'

Interviews with Heads of Department about their expectations of new pupils in Year 7

The interviews revealed a pattern of low expectation in terms of writing skills, similar to that revealed through the survey. The teachers interviewed expected new pupils in Year 7 to be able to write in sentences, to be able to use capital letters and full stops correctly and to copy accurately, though some were critical of the poor writing skills of a significant proportion of new pupils.

For example, the Head of English, Mr Rawbone, expected most new pupils to write in sentences and to be able to spell common words correctly. They should write neatly, and be able to edit and redraft their work. He expected that new pupils would be able to recognise and discuss differences between genres, for example between a newspaper report and a story.

The importance of subject content and key skills in shaping the approach to writing was evident in other interviews. The Head of Mathematics, Mr Treherne, emphasised that communicating mathematically was an important strand throughout Key Stages 3 and 4, having particular importance at GCSE, when it was one of three coursework assessment criteria strands. The writing skills that new pupils were expected to have, so that they could develop their mathematical knowledge, included:

- answering in sentences;
- copying out factual information for revision and recall;
- describing patterns in words;

- 'explain how you got your answer', e.g. finding an angle using angle facts;
- writing and reading numbers, e.g. write 1572 in words;
- learning of key words, e.g. names of shapes, or the spelling of words like 'parallel'.

These priorities were partially reflected in the survey data (Figure 5.1): writing sentences, answering questions and copying accurately were among the six general writing skills which most teachers of mathematics and science expected new pupils to have at the beginning of Year 7. Other skills, such as explaining how you got your answer, or writing a number in words, were specific to mathematics.

The writing skills that the Head of Science, Mr Harris, expected new pupils to have were the ability to:

- copy accurately from the blackboard (though 'this is not something I employ a great deal of. . .');
- write down in their own words what they see or measure in the laboratory, either in concise sentences, or filling in the appropriate part of a worksheet linked to an experiment.

In his view about 10% of new pupils lacked basic technical skills in writing. The responses of science teachers in the survey data were similar to the expectations of the Head of Science. None of the science teachers at the Spencer School completed the questionnaire, though I asked them twice through a senior teacher at the school, who was very supportive of my research.

The Head of History, Mr Dear, also assumed a level of 'basic literacy', and these expectations were also reflected in the survey data (Figure 5.1), where all (or nearly all) the humanities teachers expected pupils to be able to use full stops correctly, to copy accurately, to use capital letters, answer questions and use a dictionary. At primary school new pupils had (for example) studied the Victorians or the Romans, but Mr Dear's view was that they lacked the understanding of historical concepts and terminology (e.g. 'artefacts', 'chronology'). Teachers had to ensure that the pupils had the appropriate literacy skills, so that they could use these concepts in their written work.

In geography, on the other hand, assessing pupils' knowledge required short, concise answers. The expectation in the first term of Year 7 was that pupils would be able to write a single sentence to answer a question, or use a cloze test. Pupils were not expected to write a single paragraph about a particular topic. The survey data also showed that the majority of humanities teachers expected new pupils to answer questions and to be able to write in sentences.

Thus there was broad agreement between the teachers about the need for new pupils in Year 7 to have basic writing skills, though different types of writing were needed to be successful across the curriculum. These differences between subjects became evident when curriculum continuity between Key Stages 2 and 3 was discussed.

Perceptions of Key Stage 2

From a curriculum point of view, most of the Heads of Department I interviewed were critical of the lack of an adequate grounding that pupils received in most subjects at Key Stage 2. For example, in history and geography, the first part of the autumn term in Year 7 was used to give pupils the concepts and skills that would enable them to benefit from the Key Stage 3 courses. In mathematics, the beginning of the course was a form of revision and consolidation to ensure that all pupils started from the same baseline of knowledge and skills.

All the Heads of Department were distrustful of the Key Stage 2 National Curriculum assessments, and considered that either they were likely to be inaccurate, or of little use in planning the start of the Key Stage 3 curriculum. This commonly held view also reinforced their expectations of writing. These expectations were low (in terms of basic literacy), but they were also informed by the knowledge of the writing skills that pupils would need to be successful at Key Stages 3 and 4.

Teachers' views on what was a good piece of writing in their subject

The analysis of the survey data in answer to this question is presented in two frequency tables, Tables 5.1 and 5.2. Table 5.1 shows that most emphasis was placed on using writing to demonstrate knowledge and understanding (64%), and linked to this was the expectation that good writing would demonstrate clarity of expression (63%), logical progression (44%), coherent structure (37%) and factual accuracy (37%). Creativity, innovative ideas, and the ability to empathise had low frequency scores, though there were some anomalies. For example, the ability to be objective had a score of 14%, under half of the score for factual accuracy.

Differences emerged between the different subjects when the scores for columns 1 ('very important') and 2 (the next down on the scale of importance) were combined in Table 5.2. The differences reflected the

Table 5.1 All teachers: your view of a good piece of writing in your subject. Frequency of scores from very important (=1) through to unimportant (=5)

Score	1	2	3	4	5
Creativity	10 (17%)	13 (22%)	9 (15%)	8 (14%)	5 (85%)
Clarity of expression	37 (63%)	11 (19%)	6 (10%)	0	0
Logical progression	26 (44%)	11 (19%)	12 (20%)	2 (3%)	2 (3%)
Factual accuracy	22 (37%)	14 (24%)	10 (17%)	3 (5%)	3 (5%)
Innovative ideas	7 (12%)	17 (29%)	14 (24%)	9 (15%)	4 (7%)
Expression of writer's feelings or point of view	15 (25%)	14 (24%)	10 (17%)	4 (7%)	6 (10%)
Development of an argument	12 (20%)	12 (20%)	11 (19%)	3 95%)	7 (12%)
Good introduction	13 (22%)	14 (23%)	11 (19%)	4 (7%)	6 (10%)
Good conclusion	18 (31%)	13 (22%)	9 (15%)	3 (5%)	6 (10%)
Coherent structure	22 (37%)	21 (36%)	4 (7%)	0	4 (7%)
Ability to empathise	9 (15%)	15 (25%)	7 (12%)	6 (10%)	11 (19%)
Ability to be objective	8 (14%)	20 (34%)	11 (19%)	3 (5%)	5 (9%)
Demonstrate knowledge and understanding	38 (64%)	11 (19%)	5 (9%)	0	0
Accurate spelling	14 (24%)	22 (37%)	15 (25%)	4 (7%)	0
Correct use of paragraphing	5 (9%)	19 (32%)	12 (20%)	6 (10%)	2 (3%)
Use of standard English	15 (25%)	14 (24%)	12 (20%)	2 (3%)	3 (5%)

1. Total number of teachers in the sample = 59
2. All percentages have been rounded up or down.

Table 5.2 All teachers of English, mathematics, science, history and geography: your view of what is important in a good piece of writing in your subject

	English (12)	Mathematics (7)	Science (4)	History (3)	Geography (4)
Creativity	12	1	0	1	1
Clarity of expression	12	3	4	3	3
Logical progression	6	5	4	3	3
Factual accuracy	4	5	4	3	4
Innovative ideas	9	2	2	2	1
Expression of writer's feelings or point of view	11	0	0	1	1
Development of an argument	8	3	1	3	3
Good introduction	9	3	2	2	2
Good conclusion	5	4	4	3	3
Coherent structure	11	3	4	3	3
Ability to empathise	10	1	0	1	4
Ability to be objective	7	0	0	3	3
Demonstrate knowledge and understanding	8	5	4	3	4
Accurate spelling	8	5	1	1	2
Correct use of paragraphing	9	2	0	3	3
Use of standard English	7	2	2	2	4

1. Numbers in brackets denote total numbers of teachers.
2. Survey returns from science and history teachers at Jeremy Priestley School only.
3. Frequency of scores 1 + 2 (very important plus important) on the scale 1–5

types of writing that were most valued in different subject areas. For example, all or nearly all the English teachers thought the following features were most important in good writing: creativity, clarity of expression, expression of a writer's feelings or viewpoint, coherent structure and the ability to empathise. By contrast, the features of good writing identified as most important by the majority of the mathematics teachers were: logical progression, factual accuracy, demonstration of knowledge and understanding, and correct spelling. The comments of individual teachers about good writing reflected priorities in different subjects, for example:

> Mathematics teacher: (Reflecting on his answers to the question about good writing) 'Thinking here mainly of coursework tasks, say, the ability to write a report about an investigation.'

> ADT teacher: 'Students' ability to systematically analyse and select information when producing an evaluation of their own work or another artist's. Research skills – mostly in written form and done with clarity.'

> Geography teacher: 'A good factual correct piece of writing using standard correct English. I always use this sentence – too often – "PLEASE WRITE IN FULL SENTENCES." I sometimes wonder whether anyone, anywhere, explains this to them when answering questions.'

The interview data also revealed how notions of good writing were determined by the uses of writing within the subject. For example, Mr Rawbone, the Head of English at Jeremy Priestley School, considered that good writing (in whatever genre) would be characterised by a clear sense of audience and purpose, with a varied and appropriate vocabulary. There would be a high standard of accuracy in spelling, and correct punctuation would be used.

In mathematics, there were two main strands which characterised the uses of writing: the need to provide brief, crisp explanations or answers, and the ability to develop a more 'narrative' approach at GCSE, when the pupil was expected to provide an explanation of how a problem was solved. Thus for Mr Treherne, the Head of Mathematics, the notion of good writing included:

- writing that was clearly understood;
- short, precise sentences;

- crisp explanantions;
- the use of narrative to supply a running commentary of the thoughts of the pupils as s/he developed an idea (needed at GCSE);
- writing that was broken up with diagrams, photos and images 'to stimulate, intrigue and offer pause for thought'.

These categories are not identical with those identified as most important in the survey (Table 5.2). For example, clarity of expression was regarded as very important by only three out of seven mathematics teachers, even though the Head of Mathematics considered 'writing that is clearly understood' as the first of five factors characterising 'good writing'. This is because the survey used a limited number of categories which all teachers had to respond to, whereas in interview the subject specialists could use whatever categories they felt were most appropriate for their subject.

In science there was an emphasis on writing which enabled one to record facts, and this was contrasted by Mr Harris, the Head of Science, with English where 'you express yourselves'. The recording of facts could involve using a set format for writing up an experiment, or tabulating results in a chart or table.

The main features of good writing in history, according to Mr Dear, the Head of History, were:

- factual accuracy;
- use of the correct terminology;
- writing that was linked to the production of a well-structured essay.

In Table 5.2 we can see that all the history teachers considered that factual accuracy, logical progression, clarity of expression, the development of an argument, a coherent structure and a good conclusion were very important in good writing in history – features which would be found in a well-structured essay.

The Head of Geography, Mr Wilson, considered the main purpose of writing in his subject was to convey information concisely, and this was particularly important at GCSE. He cited with approval a geography teacher at university who refused to mark an answer beyond the twelfth word, as an example of conciseness. He explained that he often said to pupils that 'what applies to geography is what I tell you, and even if geographical sentences are short and blunt and don't sound very nice, they might be bad for English, but they are good for geography.'

In general, the survey and interview data show areas of agreement, and highlight that the notion of good writing was determined by the cognitive demands and assessment needs of the particular subject, and that these needs differed between subjects. However, teachers' expectations of the writing skills most pupils would possess at the beginning of Year 7 were lower than those described for writing at Level 4 in English. For example, at Level 4 pupils' writing in a range of forms is 'lively and thoughtful'. Ideas are developed in 'interesting ways', and pupils are beginning to use 'grammatically complex sentences, extending meaning'. Spelling is generally accurate, and 'full stops, capital letters and question marks are used correctly' (DfE 1995a: 30). It should also be noted that in the Key Stage 2 tests in 1997 (when the target pupils took the tests) 60% of pupils achieved Level 4 or above for writing (QCA 1998b: 3). My data show that teachers in Year 7 had lower expectations of the writing skills of new pupils, compared to the national picture of pupils' achievements in writing at the end of Key Stage 2. The implications of this for teaching and learning at the beginning of Key Stage 3 will be discussed in Chapter 8.

The types of writing pupils did in Year 7 lessons, and the sorts of writing mistakes teachers corrected

From the survey, there was a difference between the types of writing which English teachers said took place in their lessons, and the perceptions of other teachers. In English lessons the commonest types of writing activity involved different types of fiction (Figure 5.2), such as stories, plays and poems. In other subjects copying, summarising and answering questions were among the most frequently identified types of writing. Answering questions was identified by the majority of teachers as the writing activity which occurred most frequently in their lessons. Other writing activities identified by over half the teachers in the survey were copying off the board, summarising, brainstorming, labelling, note-taking and writing reports.

On the other hand, the mathematics teachers identified copying from the blackboard or a textbook, labelling, and answering questions as the most frequently occurring writing activities in their lessons (Figure 5.2). The Head of Mathematics, Mr Treherne, identified the following types of writing that he thought occurred most frequently in Year 7 mathematics lessons:

- writing answers in sentences;
- copying out factual information;

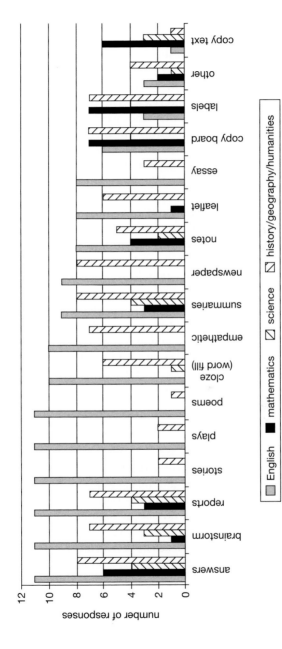

Figure 5.2 What types of writing do Year 7 pupils produce in your lessons?

- copying out a definition;
- describing number patterns in words, e.g. 'to move from one number to the next you have to multiply by 3 and add 7';
- explaining how you got your answer – this could be in the form of bullet points, not necessarily in complete sentences.

Answering questions in sentences and copying were identified both in the survey data and in the interview. The types of writing activities described by the Head of Mathematics were linked to the teaching of definitions and concepts, and testing knowledge and understanding.

From the survey, the science teachers identified the most frequent writing activities as: summarising, writing reports, copying off the board, answering questions and labelling. In the humanities, on the other hand, the three most frequent types of writing identified in the survey were the writing of summaries and newspaper reports, and answering questions (Figure 5.2).

A number of additional writing activities were identified by teachers in other subjects. For example, one teacher of French commented that her pupils 'write down what they hear; copy words and sentences; captions to pictures; attempting to recognise parts of speech and fit them into text via cloze procedure'. Another colleague identified 'posters with labels'. Writing evaluations of projects ('using a prompt sheet') was identified by one ADT teacher and one design and technology teacher. One music teacher stated that her pupils wrote 'free responses to extracts of music'. These examples indicated the range of writing activities that took place in some Year 7 lessons, depending on the subject.

The mistakes teachers corrected in pupils' work

From the survey data, there was considerable agreement about the writing mistakes that were corrected. The most commonly corrected writing mistake was spelling, and mistakes in the use of capital letters and full stops were also corrected in all subjects (Figure 5.3). Correcting mistakes in grammar appeared to occur slightly more often in English lessons than in other subjects.

The written comments of teachers revealed considerable sensitivity to the needs of the individual pupil. The response of a teacher of religious studies was typical of many: 'Corrections would depend on a student's needs and ability, i.e. I would not correct every error made by a student with significant spelling difficulties.' An ADT teacher wrote that she would penalise faulty grammar 'only where no sense can be made of a sentence'. The effect of teaching for GCSE on priorities at Key Stage

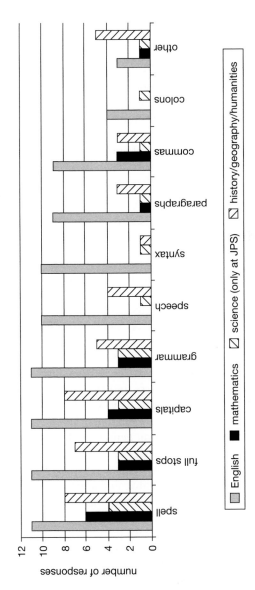

Figure 5.3 What writing mistakes do you correct in your pupils' work (by subject)?

3 were revealed by one teacher of mathematics who commented, 'I do take more time with a GCSE coursework practice task, where paragraphing and (the) general structure of a piece of work are important.'

This picture was reflected, more or less, in the interviews. For example, the Head of Geography (Mr Wilson) tried to pre-empt certain common spelling mistakes of technical terms: 'sometimes I say to a class that we're about to do earthquakes, not earthquacks and we have a little giggle about a common spelling mistake, and I tell them about Ron who lives in the middle of environment, because many of them miss out the "n".' Though there was not enough time for pupils to copy out their corrections, the correction of spelling mistakes occurred largely because the key terms were used to teach basic concepts, for example 'chronology' in history or 'weather' in geography.

Techniques and approaches used to teach different genres of writing

The National Literacy Strategy has given primary and secondary teachers a shared framework for the teaching of writing (e.g. DfEE 2001b). What I want to analyse in this section is the genres teachers were using in Year 7, and the techniques employed to teach them in 1998 – three years before the NLS was introduced into secondary schools. This will provide a contrast with the discussion in Chapter 6, which is based on interviews conducted with teachers in 2002.

The most striking difference in the survey data was between the genres taught by English teachers and the rest. All English teachers taught pupils how to write stories, plays and reports, and the majority taught the writing of poems, newspapers, letters, personal writing and essays. The writing of fiction genres predominated (Figure 5.4). When all teachers are considered, the most frequently taught genres were reports, followed by newspapers, personal writing (recounts), letters and note-taking. Mathematics and science teachers placed most emphasis on teaching pupils to write reports, while in humanities, newspapers, reports, essays and note-taking were the types of writing most commonly taught (Figure 5.4).

The most important techniques used to teach the writing of different genres were verbal instruction, followed by the use of instructions on the blackboard, modelling, brainstorming and the use of worksheets (Table 5.3).

There were differences between different subject areas in the ways genres were taught, as shown in Table 5.4. In English, verbal instruction,

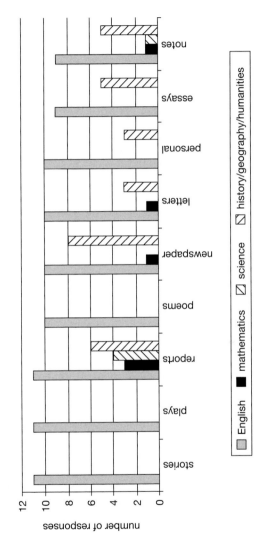

Figure 5.4 Genres taught in your Year 7 lessons (by subject)

Table 5.3 All teachers: techniques used to teach the writing of different genres

Score	1	2	3	4	5
Verbal instruction	28	11	3		
	48%	18%	5%		
Instructions on blackboard	15	17	4	1	
	25%	29%	7%	2%	
Instructions in text book	5	9	13	3	6
	9%	15%	22%	5%	10%
Worksheet	13	13	10	2	1
	22%	22%	17%	3%	2%
Brainstorming	18	12	5	2	2
	35%	20%	9%	3%	3%
Modelling	14	11	5	5	
	23%	19%	9%	9%	
Scaffolding	8	16	6	4	2
	14%	27%	10%	7%	3%
Editing	12	8	6	4	2
	20%	14%	10%	7%	3%
Redrafting	12	10	9	2	2
	20%	17%	15%	3%	3%

1. Total number of teachers in sample = 55
2. All percentages rounded up or down
3. Frequency of scores from 'very important' (=1) to 'unimportant' (=5)

redrafting, editing and brainstorming were the most favoured techniques, though individual teachers developed their own approaches. The Head of English at Jeremy Priestley School had circulated writing frames for the teaching of non-fiction writing from the EXEL project (Lewis and Wray 1998), and members of the department had started to produce more writing frames of their own, particularly for literature essays at Key Stage 3.

According to the survey data, the techniques most favoured by mathematics teachers for the teaching of genres were verbal instruction, followed by instructions on the board and from a textbook. Mr Treherne, the Head of Mathematics, used the following techniques and approaches to teach different writing skills:

- by example (modelling);
- through class discussion, e.g. 'who can spell?', 'who can write this on the board?';

Table 5.4 Strategies used to teach the writing of different genres in English, mathematics, science, history and geography

	English (12)	Mathematics (7)	Science (4)	History (3)	Geography (4)
Verbal instruction	12	3	4	3	3
Instructions on board	8	2	4	3	3
Instructions in text book	2	2	3		1
Worksheet	7	2	4	1	2
Brainstorming	10	1		2	2
Modelling	9	1	2		1
Scaffolding	6		1	3	3
Editing	11		1	1	
Redrafting	12		1		

1. Numbers in brackets denote the number of subject teachers
2. Completed surveys from science and history teachers from Jeremy Priestley School only.
3. Frequency of scores 1(=very important) plus 2 (=important) on the scale 1–5

- developing confidence to talk mathematics, e.g. 'I am a Martian, describe a square to me';
- by challenging every ambiguous phrase used by pupils, so that they could see the need for clear thought and speech;
- spelling tests to reinforce the spelling of technical terms.

The most favoured techniques used by science teachers to teach the writing of genres were verbal instruction, instructions on the board, and worksheets. In Year 7 pupils used a science textbook, which provided the structure for the course, and gave them opportunities for recording and interpreting data in the standard manner.

Mr Dear, the Head of History, explained that there was a carefully planned programme at the beginning of Year 7 to teach concepts and language skills. The initial activities involved answering questions with short sentences. Then the pupils moved on to writing paragraphs, through work on descriptions, such as describing Maiden Castle. Key concepts would be introduced, such as rampart and ditch, etc. The next stage would be empathy work, for example, 'Imagine you are a Roman soldier or a Celt at Maiden Castle'. The pupils would be encouraged to write at greater length in paragraphs, using a word list to provide the appropriate vocabulary. This approach prepared the pupils for learning how to write an argumentative essay, as described in Chapter 4.

By contrast, the emphasis in Year 7 geography was on producing concise, short answers or filling in missing words to demonstrate understanding and knowledge. Highly structured writing frames were sometimes used with Year 7 pupils, which were 'not much beyond word fill' or the completion of a sentence. For example, in a project on teleworking writing frames were used to enable pupils to write about the advantages and disadvantages by completing paragraphs. Those pupils who went on to take GCSE geography were required to communicate knowledge and understanding as clearly as possible in the exam, making one statement per sentence. Thus, the requirements of the GCSE examination at the end of Year 11 had a determining effect on the types of writing that pupils were expected to produce lower down the school. We can see from this section that a range of approaches was used to teach the types of writing required to be successful in different subjects.

Primary school – interview with Mr Taylor

The types of writing pupils produced in Mr Taylor's lessons

The acquisition of technical skills such as spelling, punctuation and paragraphing, the use of correct grammar, neat handwriting, and the importance of writing narrative for the Key Stage 2 tests, were emphasised by Mr Taylor. His idea of 'good' writing was expressed in terms of the content, use of interesting vocabulary, sentence structure, correct paragraphing, and whether the pupils had picked out 'the idea of the lesson'.

The importance of the Key Stage 2 tests surfaced during the interview several times. Mr Taylor commented on the pressure that teachers experienced in Year 6 to ensure that pupils got good Key Stage 2 test results, for example Level 4, because the league tables were published in the local paper. Preparation for the English test usually took two months, starting in the spring term, though it was combined with the topic work. 'We're talking about it (the tests) every day, I'd say it would come up in some aspect of our teaching.' Mr Taylor had recommended published study guides for English, mathematics and science to parents, though it was 'mainly the middle-class parents' who were interested in buying them. These expectations also explain the emphasis placed on the teaching of narrative in Year 6, as part of the preparation for the SATs, even though other genres were taught and used. He was proud of his pupils' achievements in the Key Stage 2 tests, but he had not received any information about the types of writing his pupils would be expected to do at the secondary school.

Techniques and approaches to the teaching of writing

Mr Taylor followed a textbook for Key Stage 2 published by Stanley Thornes when teaching narrative. In the autumn term of Year 6 he would start by teaching the pupils about the settings of stories, and getting them to write a couple of paragraphs about where a story took place. The pupils would then study character, and write a character study. This would be followed by studying the structure of a story, concentrating on good openings, the middle part and the ending. 'So it's all a long, long process and then we hope the half term, when we come to the half term before the SATs, we can go onto that and it will pick up and we can put it all together then'.

Pupils would have timed practices, and Mr Taylor would put a level on a test piece if the pupil had achieved Level 4 or 5 to encourage them. Sometimes he would discuss with pupils what was required to achieve a Level 4 for a piece of writing, for example in terms of improving vocabulary, descriptions or punctuation.

Discussion

Both survey and interview data showed that most secondary teachers felt they had a role in teaching pupils to write in ways that were appropriate for their subject, so that pupils could learn new concepts and skills, and demonstrate their knowledge. However, the pupils' curriculum experiences (including writing) in the primary school, including the Key Stage 2 test results, were not valued by their teachers in Year 7. It would appear that Mr Taylor's views and practices reflected higher expectations of the writing skills of pupils at the end of Year 6 than many of the secondary school teachers had at the beginning of Year 7. In spite of over ten years of the National Curriculum, there was little communication between the primary and secondary teachers about the teaching and uses of writing. The implications for continuity and progression at primary–secondary transfer will be discussed in the next chapter.

Implications for the practising teacher

- How do you understand the notions of 'good' writing and 'better' writing in your subject?
- How do you conceptualise the notion of progression in writing in your subject, and how do you communicate this understanding to your pupils?
- Use the summary grid about 'good' and 'better' writing from Chapter 6 (Table 6.1) at a staff INSET session, and ask teachers to complete it and discuss similarities and differences in cross-curricular groups. What emerges from this activity about whole-school approaches to improving pupils' writing?
- What features of pupils' writing do you tend to focus on when talking to pupils about improving their writing, and what techniques do you favour? Do you think your approach has changed as a result of the NLS, or are you are using the same techniques as (say) five or six years ago? Are these techniques similar to those used by other teachers in your department, or in other departments? How could you find out?
- Discuss with your pupils what they understand by 'good' writing, and ask them how they would advise another pupil (in the same year, or a younger pupil) how s/he could improve their writing. If you teach a Year 7 class, you could ask your pupils to provide this advice for pupils in Year 6. It could be expressed in the form of a letter, a spider diagram or a series of bullet points. Would they give the same advice to another pupil about improving his/her writing in (say) science or history as in English? If there are differences, what are they, and how do pupils explain them?
- Is there a difference or a disjunction between the ways you conceptualise 'good' writing and 'better' writing (i.e. progression), and the conceptualisations of your pupils? This is an important question, as I discussed in Chapter 4, because if there is a disjunction, then the pupils' interpretations of a writing task may be different from the teacher's.
- What targets do you tend to share with the whole class and with individual pupils for the improvement of their writing? If you analyse the targets that you use with the majority of your pupils, are there a few that you use most of the time (e.g. 'correct spelling', 'write in more detail')? Do you teach or model what (say) 'writing in more detail' means?
- What opportunities do you give pupils to review and record their progress in writing, e.g. through the use of their own 'Progress Records' and targets negotiated with the teacher?

6 Joining the dance: literacy update 2002

'The further off from England the nearer is to France –
Then turn not pale, beloved snail, but come and join the dance. . .'
Alice's Adventures in Wonderland, Chapter 10.

When the Mock Turtle sang these words he may unwittingly have been invoking notions of progression by identifying an objective, in spite of the snail's anxiety that the proposed journey was 'Too far, too far!' We have all joined this particular dance without any choice, and some of us have turned pale when considering its cost in terms of time and resources. The key questions about the National Literacy Strategy which I will attempt to answer in this chapter are whether it has changed teachers' expectations and ideals about writing in Years 6 and 7, and whether it has enhanced continuity and progression between the secondary and primary school in this case study.

In May 2002 I re-interviewed the teachers who participated in the original case study. If they had left the schools involved, I interviewed their replacements, using many of the questions from 1997/98. As you might expect, the picture that emerged was a complex one. From the analysis of these interviews I will:

- discuss the benefits of the NLS with reference to the teaching of writing;
- identify the features that do not appear to have changed much in the space of four years;
- comment on the effects of the NLS on continuity and progression.

In Chapter 8 I will link this section to my discussion of what teachers can do to promote continuity and progression between primary and secondary phases.

Teachers' expectations and ideals about writing in Year 7

The writing skills that Heads of Department expected new pupils to have at the beginning of Year 7

In general, the expectations of the Heads of Department that I interviewed had not changed much since the original interviews, and I checked this by reading out their comments from the first interviews. For example, the Head of Mathematics, Mr Treherne, had become an Assistant Headteacher; the writing expectations he had of new pupils were much the same as before. His replacement, Mr Speedwell (formerly the Second-in-Department) felt that new pupils should be able to write in sentences, and to use bullet points to present a written commentary. By the end of Year 7 most pupils were expected to produce a structured report on a piece of investigative work with an introduction and three paragraphs.

The Head of Science, Mr Harris, didn't change what he had said four years before, though he felt that the average and above average new pupils now had better writing skills. The expectations of Mr Rawbone, the Head of English, were similar to those in 1997/98, and he focused on technical skills, and editing and redrafting. He felt that many pupils in Year 7 responded well to the use of modelling, writing frames and starter sentences to support their writing, because they were familiar with these approaches from the primary school as a result of the Literacy Hour.

Mr Wilson, the Head of Geography, had not noticed an appreciable change in the writing skills of new pupils, compared to four years before, in spite of the NLS at primary school. The new Head of History, Ms Green, had joined the school two years after I had interviewed her predecessor, Mr Dear. Ms Green identified the following writing skills she expected new pupils to have: the ability to write in sentences, and to 'put down what they are thinking' on paper. Ms Green felt that up to a quarter of new pupils had very weak literacy skills. This would 'seriously stop them in their learning and in expressing their learning on paper. They might be able to do it orally but getting it into written form was very difficult for them.'

The views of Heads of Department on what was a good piece of writing in their subject

Had the views of the teachers I interviewed about what constituted 'good writing' in their subject changed appreciably since 1997/98, that is, since the introduction of the NLS? In general, the teachers' accounts of the writing demands in each subject in Year 7 in 2002 were broadly similar to those I observed in 1997/98, because much of the curriculum was the same (in spite of the introduction of new National Curriculum Orders in 2000). What had changed were the strategies or techniques that departments were starting to use to teach writing, which I will discuss in the next section.

The Head of Science, Mr Harris, emphasised the importance of conciseness in good writing in science, particularly in the way pupils wrote down their observations, using presentational devices such as bullet points and numbered statements. The Head of English and the Head of Geography both felt that their respective notions of good writing were basically unchanged since 1998. Ms Green, the new Head of History, emphasised the importance of clarity in good writing in history, with 'one particular point being made and explained before the pupil moves on to the next thing'. On the other hand, she felt that there was sometimes a tension between the pupil demonstrating his/her subject knowledge and understanding, but not using basic writing conventions such as full stops. For example, one pupil wrote a detailed empathetic piece (about a Roman soldier) with no punctuation marks:

> 'but what he was writing from a history point of view was quite valuable, because he's used what he'd learned. . . he'd really thought about it and tried to get the feelings and ideas of what a soldier would have felt like at the time.'

For Ms Towers, the Literacy Co-ordinator (who taught English at Key Stage 3), good writing meant improving technical skills, and giving pupils opportunities to develop their ideas through editing and redrafting, and using the different formats (genres) from the English Framework and the NLS. Ms Towers taught pupils to focus more on writing opening paragraphs or sentences in Year 7, so that they could develop ideas. This process would enable pupils to develop 'their artistry really, not just their skills', and this would benefit their extended writing.

How would you help pupils to produce 'better writing'?

I had not asked the teachers in the original case study how they would help pupils to write 'better', that is, what they thought counted as progression in writing in their subject, but I did in the follow-up interviews in 2002. The range of responses was linked to the different functions that writing had in each subject areas, and some responses reflected the influence of the Key Stage 3 Strategy. Responses from the Heads of Mathematics, Science and Geography are summarised in Table 6.1, as examples of the ways 'good' and 'better' writing were conceptualised in different subject areas.

For example, in mathematics 'better' writing included writing a clear introduction in a report, with the emphasis on precision, and pupils got more marks for doing this well. To produce a better report, in Mr Treherne's view, pupils had to make sure it was 'not waffle', but was presented in a logical sequence using bullet points. A sample of good reports from previous years was kept and shown to pupils so that they could see what was expected.

Mr Speedwell (the current Head of Mathematics) considered that 'writing better' in mathematics meant 'answering the question in full . . . not necessarily in full sentences'. The focus was on the investigational tasks the pupils wrote about; better writing meant 'have they managed to push the boundaries of their own understanding?' In Year 7 this could be demonstrated, for example, by writing their report of the 'Gardener's Walk' project (discussed below) as a story, as if they were the gardener. Mr Harris, the Head of Science, was planning to provide a series of model answers to help pupils improve their writing. Better writing occurred when ideas were expressed concisely, using numbered or bullet points, in the present tense, and technical words were spelt correctly.

For the Head of English, producing better writing meant encouraging pupils to think about audience and purpose; to improve the structure and vocabulary of their sentences; and to use editing and redrafting to develop their ideas. Presenting pupils with examples of good writing (e.g. published texts, other pupils' work), and the teacher modelling writing, were also used to promote better writing.

In geography, writing frames and starter sentences (or the beginnings of sentences) were used to help pupils improve their writing. To produce better writing in history pupils had to demonstrate their understanding, include evidence to support their views, and spell technical words correctly. Ms Green (the Head of History) would have helped the pupil who wrote an empathetic piece about a Roman soldier without

Table 6.1 Year 7: three views of 'good' writing and 'better' writing at the secondary school.
In general, the writing demands at Key Stage 3 were similar in 1998 and 2002; however, the approaches used had changed.

Subject (interview with HoD)	What do understand by 'good' writing in your subject?	How do you teach 'good' writing in your subject?	What do you understand by 'better' writing in your subject	Comments
Mathematics	• Writing that was clearly understood. • Short, precise sentences. • Crisp explanations. • The use of narrative to supply a running commentary of the thoughts of a pupil as s/he developed an idea (needed at GCSE). • Writing that was broken up with diagrams, photos and images 'to stimulate, intrigue and offer pause for thought'. (Same in 1998 and 2002.)	• Use of starter cards for different sections of report e.g. 'Gardener's Walk' project. • Clear structure for the report was provided by the teacher, plus modelling on whiteboard. • SEN staff broke task down into smaller steps and provided a booklet to help weaker students (widely used by mathematics teachers). • Standardised approach used (introduced with NLS).	• Writing a clear introduction in a report, with the emphasis on precision, and pupils got more marks for doing this well. • Pupils had to make sure the report was 'not waffle', but was presented in a logical sequence using bullet points. • A sample of good reports from previous years was kept and shown to pupils so that they could see what was expected.	Similar findings about 'good' writing in mathematics in the survey conducted among secondary teachers. Technical words displayed in mathematics classrooms.
Science	• Writing which enabled one to record facts. • Contrasted with English where 'you express yourselves'. • The recording of facts could involve using a set	• In 1998 there was a flexible approach to writing up experiments in Year 7; for some teachers recounts were acceptable if the pupils demonstrated understanding.	• The Head of Science was planning to provide a series of model answers to help pupils improve their writing. • Better writing occurred when ideas were expressed concisely, using numbered or	Lists of technical words displayed in science classrooms.

continued

Table 6.1 (continued)

Subject (interview with HoD)	What do you understand by 'good' writing in your subject?	How do you teach 'good' writing in your subject?	What do you understand by 'better' writing in your subject?	Comments
	format for writing up an experiment, or tabulating results in a chart or table	• A standardised approach was adopted for the writing of Science reports, using writing frames, technical vocabulary (in 2002). • This resulted from collaboration between the Literacy Consultant and the Science Department.	bullet points, in the present tense. • The spelling of technical words was important, and mistakes were corrected.	
Geography	• Conveys information concisely. • To pupils: 'What applies to geography is what I tell you, and even if geographical sentences are short and blunt, and don't sound very nice, they might be bad for English but they are good for Geography.' • Notion of 'good writing' the same in 1998 and 2002.	• Focus on teaching persuasive writing in Year 7. • Pupils studied the characteristics of persuasive writing (speech on mobile phones). • Pupils used a writing frame and appropriate vocabulary to argue a point of view, based on a case study. This development was a direct result of the NLS.	• Writing frames and starter sentences (or the beginning of sentences) used to help pupils improve their writing.	No noticeable improvement in pupils' writing skills in geography at the start of Year 7 since the introduction of the NLS in primary schools.

punctuation or paragraphing by reviewing with him the five headings that pupils had been given at the beginning of this task. She would have advised him to use each heading as the starting point for a new paragraph, which should have contained new information or evidence, in correctly punctuated sentences.

For Ms Towers better writing meant focusing on technical skills, and enabling pupils 'to extend their writing quite quickly, to let them see success . . . for example, use a thesaurus to develop their vocabulary.' Ms Towers often said to pupils, 'Don't write more, let's look at the bit you've got and try to make that better.' She encouraged pupils to think about improving vocabulary and sentence structure by sharing ideas with a partner.

The impact of the National Literacy Strategy on the teaching of writing in Year 7

Had the NLS made a difference to the teaching and uses of writing in Year 7? At the Jeremy Priestley School the whole-school initiative was launched in September 2001; after two terms the teachers I interviewed felt it had had an impact on teaching and learning, though the messages were mixed.

For example, when I interviewed Mr Treherne and Mr Speedwell about supporting children's writing in mathematics, we talked mainly about the 'Gardener's Walk' project in Year 7. This was an investigative assignment; the pupils had to use red and grey coloured slabs and investigate patterns which they developed from the smallest to the largest L-shape, and work out the rules that determined how many slabs were needed. When I interviewed Mr Treherne four years before, this project was taught then but there was not a consistent approach across the department as to how the pupils should write their reports. The NLS had enabled the department to adopt a shared approach. The report was divided into different sections, and coloured cards with starter sentences for different sections of the report, were set out at the front of the class. Pupils could choose a card when they were ready to start a particular section.

This technique had been developed by a member of the department working with the Literacy Co-ordinator, and it had been used success-fully for three months. The department preferred to use starter cards rather than a writing frame, because the latter was felt to be too rigid. However some pupils found this approach too difficult, for example, sequencing the different sections of the report. For those pupils the Special Needs Department had produced a booklet which broke down writing the sections of the report into small tasks, and this was widely used.

The NLS had enhanced teachers' awareness of the techniques that could be used in the classroom, and had given both teachers and pupils a greater awareness of where English (spoken and written) came into mathematics. The assessment framework within the department identified the features of the report for which pupils would get marks. Mr Treherne thought that new pupils were completing the written tasks, such as the 'Gardener's Walk' report, better than a few years before. Mr Speedwell's view was that the Literacy and Numeracy strategies had produced a much more interactive approach to teaching and learning in the classroom. As a result, 'spoken vocabulary and discussion are much better than it has been for many a year, but whether we can maintain that high level is another thing.'

In science the NLS had enabled the department to produce a writing frame for an experiment on boiling water, which would act as a model for writing up other experiments. The sheet provided key sentences and key words, and there were detailed Teachers' Notes. One feature of the writing frame was that pupils were expected to write the method in the present tense, and to record the results concisely in the past tense. This writing frame, which had been generated at a departmental meeting, had been used successfully, and more such writing frames were being planned, including one to support pupils' research in the school library. The Teachers' Notes had been created jointly by Mr Harris and the Literacy Co-ordinator. In terms of the teaching of writing in Year 7, Mr Harris felt that the Science Department had moved on compared to 1997/98.

The Head of English, Mr Rawbone, felt that there were many positive features of the English Framework at Key Stage 3; in particular it made teachers think more about their teaching objectives and the pace of lessons. Members of the English Department used starter activities, and taught the features of fiction and non-fiction texts, using modelling, much more explicitly than in 1997/98. All units of the Year 7 curriculum were being rewritten to align them with the English Framework. However, he did not want the Framework to become a straitjacket that stifled creativity in the classroom, and careful monitoring would be required to establish how classroom practice had actually changed. The department felt that the advice from the Literacy Consultant had been valuable.

In geography a new unit on persuasive writing had been developed in Year 7. The focus was a case study about whether a city in Russia should continue to specialise in mining coal and producing steel, or whether it should close them down and change to something different. The pupils had to write a persuasive piece based on the evidence, and the teacher used a number of techniques. Initially the pupils were shown what terms or phrases could be used in persuasive writing. Then the teacher would demonstrate the characteristics of persuasive writing by reading a speech about mobile phones being a bad thing. The pupils had to put up their hands when they recognised something that was characteristic of persuasive writing. At this stage they were given the case study on which they had to base their own speeches. This approach was supported by detailed Teachers' Notes, which had been developed by a member of the department.

The NLS had stimulated ways of teaching non-fiction writing in history, including the development of writing frames and starter sentences. 'Hot tips' were provided to help pupils write newspaper front pages, and existing tasks were adapted so that pupils would be taught to produce handbooks and magazines for a specific historical period. The department had moved away from the emphasis on teaching pupils to write essays, and was using a variety of written forms to assess pupils' knowledge and skills. The 'Battle of Hastings' lesson which I had observed in 1998 (see Chapter 4) had been adapted to emphasise the reasons pupils might give for choosing pieces of evidence, by giving pupils more starter sentences with which to structure their work.

For Ms Towers, who had led the whole-school initiative in her role as Literacy Co-ordinator, the biggest achievement had been to get colleagues to look at teaching and learning styles. Even though the focus had been on writing, staff had looked critically at lesson plans in the light of the NLS. Literacy across the curriculum had impinged on so many other things, and made teachers think about ways of enabling pupils to achieve higher levels in their subject. For example, the Geography Department had looked at how pupils could achieve levels 4, 5 and 6 by focusing on the writing skills that pupils needed to present geographical knowledge, and it 'is fascinating that they have been able to do that'.

The idea of modelling writing in the classroom had been a new one for many teachers, and it made them refocus their views on how to teach. Where the lead from the Head of Department had been positive, teachers were prepared to embrace the initiative, and many had already found that it made teaching their subject easier because they didn't have to focus so much on the writing activities. This was because the pupils had been taught the structures and approaches that enabled most of them to write independently. In some subjects this meant that, as a result, there was more time for practical work. The challenge for the future was to ensure that the Strategy became embedded, and that there would be a coherent approach across the school for the teaching of writing and other literacy skills.

Pupils' writing in Year 6, and its impact on writing in Year 7

The Heads of Department were, by and large, ignorant of the types of writing that new pupils had done in Year 6 in their subject, and this had not changed since 1998. Mr Harris, the Head of Science, considered that an audit was required of what was going on in science in the partnership primary schools, so that teachers at Key Stages 2 and 3 could support each other. He did not want ten different primary schools to be teaching the writing of scientific reports with ten different approaches. On the other hand, he did not want to be seen as dictating what or how they should be teaching, but felt that 'a level of consistency needs to be established'.

An attempt to create curriculum continuity in science seven years before, in conjunction with the Spencer School (the other secondary school) and local primary schools, had been not been successful. The two secondary schools had provided materials, books, equipment, other resources and expertise to set up the equivalent of bridging activities, but the primary sector 'was absolutely snowed under with assessment, record keeping, etc., and we . . . had Induction Days, an ever-changing curriculum, and the scheme just fell flat on its face. The will was there, but the time just wasn't.' Different priorities in the primary and secondary schools had affected the potential success of this initiative.

I also interviewed the Literacy Co-ordinator, Ms Towers, who had come into post in July 2001, before that she had been the Special Needs Co-ordinator (SENCO). She considered that the Literacy Strategy at Key Stage 2 had had most impact on the technical skills of some pupils, and had resulted in improved writing, particularly for boys, a view which she shared with the Head of English. Ms Towers had found that new pupils, particularly boys, had responded more confidently to writing about issues, such as bullying, when they were presented with the structured approach they were familiar with from Key Stage 2. The writing of some of these pupils was of a higher level than she would have expected. When writing was not taught in this way in Year 7, some pupils experienced difficulties.

Linked to this were two further points. First, the new pupils often found it quite difficult overall to transfer the writing skills they had been taught at primary school to the range of subjects they experienced in

Year 7. Second, Ms Towers felt interesting writing activities took place 'where you would expect them', such as in history and geography. In other subjects, such as in design technology, the teachers had very high expectations of the sorts of writing pupils should produce, even though the pupils often did not understand the context or concept of the writing required. In other subjects, on the other hand, the writing was not challenging enough, which was similar to my finding in 1997/98.

Ms Towers also taught classes in the English Department at Key Stage 3. In her opinion, since the introduction of the NLS new pupils tended to be focused on technical skills at the expense of creativity: 'Perhaps subconsciously they're focusing on the technical skills and they're not allowing their imaginations to develop'. She felt that the priority of English teachers in Year 7 should be to enable pupils to develop their ideas more imaginatively, because she felt this had not happened sufficiently at Key Stage 2. This point was also made, from a different perspective, by the two Year 6 teachers I interviewed, Ms Ellis and Ms Jones (see below).

Messages to the Minister

One person was missing during the interviews with my colleagues: the Secretary of State for Education. I asked my colleagues what they would have liked to say to the Minister about the NLS and related issues. The general comments about the NLS, and the whole-school focus on non-fiction writing, were positive, but a number of concerns came to the surface. For example, Mr Speedwell (Head of Mathematics) thought it was a good idea to teach pupils to develop their literacy skills, but his main concern was whether the initiative was going to be supported in future by the government. Mr Harris (Head of Science) thought the NLS was one of the few initiatives that was making a difference for the better. Mr Rawbone (Head of English) welcomed the best features of the NLS, though he was concerned about the workload implications of introducing the Key Stage 3 English Framework. His message was that there should be less prescription from the centre, and a greater willingness on the part of government to trust teachers' professionalism.

Mr Wilson (Head of Geography) had a number of reservations about the implementation of the Strategy at secondary school. He questioned how effective liaison between departments about the teaching of writing could be co-ordinated without increasing teachers' workload. Given the limited time available for the teaching of geography in the secondary school curriculum, he would have liked 'clearer guidance' from the Minister about what he was meant to be doing with the Strategy. He would also want to be reassured that the teaching of writing skills in geography was not being duplicated in other subjects. Ms Green's message was that there should be more resources to provide in-class support for new pupils who had very low reading and writing ages, and more time to collaborate with Special Needs colleagues in planning support for those pupils.

Ms Towers (Literacy Co-ordinator) had two messages for the Minister. The first was the issue of additional workload for staff. The second message was that some of the resources produced by government agencies, for example for the teaching of writing, or some of the Progress Units, did not take sufficient account of the sophisticated lives our pupils led. These materials often did not reflect students' interests sufficiently, and some of the Progress Units could have used ICT to be more effective. She supported the idea of Transition Units, but doubted whether staff would have the time to make them work. In general, then, the main messages were about workload, time issues and the future of the Strategy.

The Primary School – interviews with Ms Ellis and Ms Jones

I wanted to know what my primary colleagues thought about the impact of the NLS on children's writing, and the implications for continuity and progression at transition. Mr Taylor, the Year 6 teacher in the original case study, had left, so I interviewed the two Year 6 teachers in May 2002. They were Ms Ellis, who had been teaching Year 6 classes for the previous two years and was the school's Literacy Co-ordinator, and Ms Jones, who had taught Year 6 classes for five years and had experienced at first hand the effect of the NLS on Year 6 teaching. She was also the Mathematics Co-ordinator for the school.

How has the NLS changed the teaching of writing in Year 6?

In general, both teachers felt that though the NLS had given them a range of techniques for analysing and teaching writing, most of the writing which pupils produced tended to be short pieces. More time was needed to consolidate children's writing skills through extended writing.

The main opportunities that the pupils had for extended writing were the termly Writing Weeks when they had the time to edit and redraft longer pieces of work, and topic work. The period after the SATs was used mainly for topic work, which provided more opportunities for extended writing. In 1997 topic work was one of the main vehicles for the delivery of the curriculum; now it appeared almost like an oasis after the more prescriptive approaches involved in teaching the NLS, and preparation for the Key Stage 2 tests.

What types of writing do pupils produce in your lessons, and what techniques do you use to teach writing?

The types of writing which the two teachers identified were stories, newspapers, letters, reports, instructions, other non-fiction text types and radio interviews. The approaches used were in line with the NLS: short pieces of text were used to introduce a language point, or to lead on to the teaching of a genre. Analysis took place at word, sentence and text levels, and led on to the teaching of the genre. Other teaching techniques were the use of whole-class whiteboard work, class discussion, teacher modelling and pupils using whiteboards (enthusiastically) to develop their ideas. Ms Ellis had circulated materials about the types of language appropriate for different genres of writing, but she wasn't sure how extensively they were used; she did not have the time to go into colleagues' classrooms to monitor this.

The writing of newspaper front pages and radio interviews, which I had observed in Mr Taylor's classes in 1997, were still post-SATs activities. The approaches used in the classroom had changed to some extent as a result of the NLS. For example, Ms Ellis had circulated a writing frame for a front page (with spaces for headlines, picture, lead paragraph), and the 'teachers who are interested are highlighting what types of language you use, and how it differs from a normal report . . . yes, it (the NLS) has made a difference. . .' She thought that another benefit of the NLS had been that teachers were able to identify and teach the differences between (say) reports and recounts more confidently.

Ms Ellis was very pleased with the radio interviews that her class had produced after the national tests. The stimulus was a storyboard about a road accident, and the pupils had to record a news item about it. The quality of the work produced surprised her:

'They knew exactly how to speak and how to present it, because they are so used to TV broadcasts. I suddenly thought the spoken work is of much higher quality than their stories, because they don't read stories any more, and their experience of stories is very limited.'

She felt that much of the curriculum ignored the experiences of the children out of school. For example, many of her pupils didn't read at home, they watched TV or played computer games, so they didn't really understand how to make their own stories better. But when it came to a news broadcast there 'wasn't a single child who didn't understand the type of language to use, the jargon.'

A similar point was made by Ms Jones, who commented on the difficulties most of her pupils experienced with writing. The majority tended to 'write as they speak, and it is only the more able who think about what they are writing and put a lot more into it.' These tended to be the children with the wider vocabulary. She felt that experiences in the home were crucial; most pupils played computer games, watched videos, and 'there are not as many children having access to text, and their poor reading skills are beginning to hold them back across the curriculum'. The significance of home experiences, and their possible effects on children's writing, will be discussed in the next chapter.

In science, pupils were taught to write reports in a particular format, but sometimes they could simply write down facts, or produce a 'pure description'. In mathematics, a number of writing activities had been introduced during the previous two years. Pupils were given the objective for each lesson, which they had to copy down. When pupils had discovered something, for example a pattern, they were encouraged to do a bubble and write in it what they had learned. They could record their findings using bullet points, notes, sentences or whatever they felt comfortable with at that stage. If it was an investigation the pupils were expected at the end to produce a piece of written work:

> 'It backs up what they have done in their numeracy work, and it clarifies their understanding if they write in words. . . They very often write it as if they were saying it to me; most cannot make the difference between speaking and writing.'

This sounded similar to the approach used in Year 7, though without the same emphasis on producing a structured report.

In general, both teachers considered that the benefits of the NLS on children's writing were improved vocabulary and grammar. The NLS (and NNS), combined with preparation for the SATs, tended to determine the shape of the Year 6 curriculum, and non-core curriculum subjects were squeezed. Booster classes and in-class support in Year 6 tended to highlight the importance of the tests.

How do you explain the notion of 'good writing' to your pupils?

For Ms Ellis 'good writing' was writing that achieved its purpose. For example, she would explain to the pupils that if they were writing a letter, they should think about who was going to read it, whether the recipient would understand the letter, and what response they wanted. The notions of audience and purpose were difficult for many pupils, 'they're still very young and their concept of somebody reading a letter for a reason is still fairly vague'.

When Ms Jones explained good writing to her class she concentrated on word and sentence levels, using interesting vocabulary, and trying to move on from writing simple sentences to producing more complex ones. These views were not greatly different from those of Mr Taylor in 1997/98, though the techniques used to develop good writing had changed as result of the NLS.

How do you explain to pupils what writing 'better' means?

Both teachers agreed that the majority of their pupils found it difficult to understand how to write 'better'. They would identify the most important features of a child's writing that needed to be improved, and work with him/her on a one-to-one basis. The most common areas for improvement would be the use of full stops, spelling, vocabulary choices, and the use of tenses. With more able children, the discussion might be about using complex sentences to improve a description. These teachers' views about 'good' and 'better' writing are summarised in Table 6.2.

What are your expectations of the writing demands of the Year 7 curriculum?

In Year 7 Ms Ellis thought her pupils would need to be able to take notes ('more than we've actually taught them'), write more fluently and more 'skilfully' using 'different constructions in different situations'. Apart from that she considered that there was not a 'big jump' from Year 6 to Year 7, and that secondary school teachers would continue to emphasise the importance of spelling, sentence structure, paragraphing. Ms Jones felt that most of her pupils used a limited vocabulary in their writing, and that they would need to develop a wider range of vocabulary at secondary school.

Neither teacher had been given any information from the secondary school about the writing skills needed in Year 7. Ms Ellis said she would

Table 6.2 Interviews with teachers of Year 6 pupils at the adjacent primary school about 'good' and 'better' writing

Interviews with Year 6 teachers	What do you understand by 'good' writing in your subject?	How do you teach 'good' writing in your subject?	What do you understand by 'better' writing in your subject?	Comments
The Year 6 teacher whom I had worked with in 1997/98.	• Importance of spelling, punctuation and paragraphing; correct grammar and good handwriting. • Developing pupils' skills at writing narrative for the KS2 tests.	• Tended to use a KS2 textbook for the teaching of narrative	• Emphasis on technical skills.	Not much direct teaching of different genres.
The Year 6 teacher (above) had left in 2002, when I interviewed two of his colleagues.	• Writing that achieved its purpose. • Notions of audience and purpose difficult for many pupils. • Using interesting vocabulary, moving pupils from writing simple sentences to more complex ones.	• Notions of good writing not vastly different from 1997/98, but the techniques and language used to teach writing were, as a result of the NLS.	• Most pupils found it difficult to understand how to produce better writing. • The teacher would identify the most important features of a child's writing that needed to be improved, and work with him/her one-to-one. • Most common areas for improvement were: use of full stops, spelling, vocabulary choices, use of tenses. • More able pupils: taught how to use complex sentences to improve a description.	Fewer opportunities for extended writing as a result of the NLS.

find it useful to see what a Level 6 in writing in Year 7 looked like; it would give her a clearer idea of progression. Ms Jones would have liked to know what writing pupils did in mathematics in Year 7. She commented that the interactive approach of the National Numeracy Strategy in Year 7 had increased her ex-pupils' enjoyment of mathematics in the secondary school. Ms Jones felt that communication about the writing demands of different subjects in Year 7 would enable the teachers in Year 6 to prepare their pupils better for transition to the secondary school because 'it would give us another goal'.

Messages to the Minister

Ms Ellis's message to the Secretary of State for Education was that there were not enough opportunities for extended writing. There was less time for the topic work in the humanities that had given pupils a wider range of contexts in which to develop their writing. The pressure on teachers' time meant that there was too much reliance on worksheets; she felt this was not a very good technique for developing pupils' writing skills.

Ms Jones picked out two concerns. First, there should be less prescription, and the government should be prepared to trust teachers' professionalism more. Second, there should be more liaison so that primary teachers had a clearer overview of how their pupils were expected to develop at Key Stage 3. This would improve the focus of teaching at the end of Year 6.

Comment

What impressed me from the interviews was the commitment of my primary and secondary colleagues, their interest in their subject, and their willingness to explore (albeit critically) new ways of teaching. In my opinion these qualities are not sufficiently valued or recognised in the public arenas where education policy is discussed.

The National Literacy Strategy had clearly made a significant impact on the teaching of writing in Year 6, and it was starting to make an impact in Year 7, though teachers in both phases had reservations about aspects of the initiative. The main benefit of the NLS was that it made teachers think more about issues of teaching and learning.

In 2001/02 many teachers in Year 7 were using some of the same techniques as the primary teachers to teach writing, and this could be regarded as an example of unplanned continuity. However, there was virtually no communication between primary and secondary teachers about the teaching and uses of writing; in this respect the NLS had not improved continuity and progression between Years 6 and 7 compared to 1997/98. I will discuss the implications of this in more detail in Chapter 8.

Implications for the practising teacher: some successful techniques for the teaching of writing[1]

If you are a practising teacher, and you have read this chapter, you may well ask where this leaves you. Here is a checklist of techniques to promote the teaching of writing, in addition to (say) modelling and scaffolding, which teachers are already familiar with from the NLS. This list is not comprehensive, but the techniques work:

- Display key words prominently in the classroom (in lower case or with capitals as necessary), and draw attention to them.
- Key words can include technical terms which pupils should use when they deconstruct texts, before they start their own writing, e.g. bias, emotive, alliteration, puns. Boys in particular enjoy this sort of activity. As one colleague commented, 'Provide students with the tools and they'll (try to) use them.'
- Create a word wall which pupils contribute to for topics or under headings such as 'suspense', 'atmosphere', so that they can use these words in their own writing.
- Provide a clear target or targets in the lesson (this may be the main teaching objective for the lesson; explain to the class and/or put on the whiteboard). Return to these targets at the end of the lesson in your plenary.
- Use small whiteboards for pupils to experiment with opening sentences and paragraphs. Pupils can work on these individually or in pairs. The small whiteboards can also be used for spellings, which the pupils show to the teacher. S/he can then monitor any problems without identifying specific pupils.
- Provide starter sentences, differentiated writing frames or cue cards to help pupils start their writing.
- Encourage the regular, independent use of dictionaries, thesauruses and spellcheckers to help pupils develop their vocabulary. Pupils

1 I am grateful to Sarah Bowler for making detailed comments on earlier drafts of this section.

should be encouraged to experiment with new vocabulary, and praised for doing so.

- Short activities involving work on vocabulary, opening sentences, etc., should be used to boost pupils' confidence and to give them a feeling of success (this is particularly important for boys).
- Pupils should be given the opportunity to work in pairs or small groups, as appropriate, to help each other edit and improve their writing. This can be supported by the use of a checklist, and a critical friend or 'buddy'.
- Focus on writing 'better', e.g. improving the opening paragraph or the ending of a story or discursive essay, rather than writing 'more'.
- Encourage pupils, especially weak spellers or those with poor handwriting, to use ICT to produce their final drafts, which could be displayed in class.
- Set clearly attainable targets, and encourage independent learning by using (for example) in-class sheets on the rules of punctuation, which are clearly displayed with examples.
- Share with pupils examples of written work, which they have to correct and mark themselves (using National Curriculum levels). This activity could be a springboard for improving their own writing.
- Encourage pupils to take more responsibility for their own writing, and learning, across the curriculum.

7   Worlds apart? Writing in the home and writing at school

'The horror of that moment,' the King went on, 'I shall never, never forget!'

'You will, though,' the Queen said, 'if you don't make a memorandum of it.'

Alice looked on with great interest as the King took an enormous memorandum-book out of his pocket, and began writing.

Through the Looking Glass, Chapter 1.

Introduction

In this chapter I analyse the importance of home–school links with reference to writing, and relate my findings to the broader discussion about continuity and progression at primary–secondary transition. The models of writing that children experience are not, of course, limited to school, and I wanted to investigate what writing activities (typically) went on in the homes of the four target pupils. I wanted to find out what sorts of writing the adults did, how they talked about their writing activities, and whether they were able to help their children with writing tasks. I also wanted to investigate the possible influence of the types of writing that took place in the home on the pupils' attitudes and achievements where writing in school was concerned. I interviewed the parents and carers of the four target pupils in mid-July 1997 in their homes on the Windsor Estate in Billesley. The pupils had almost finished Year 6 at the Fairway Junior School. My intention was also to gain a clearer picture of the parents' understanding of school writing, and their expectations of the different writing demands that their children would experience at secondary school in the following September.

The writing activities that occurred in the home are an important part of my story. This is because the focus in primary and secondary schools tends to be on using a range of techniques to teach pupils to acquire and demonstrate writing skills, and to place the discussion of improving pupils' writing within the broad context of raising standards. What such an approach ignores, by and large, is the sophisticated nature of many pupils' lives, in terms of access to or the use of media texts through TV, video, films and computer games; the use of the Internet; the use of computers to produce and alter texts; and the transmission of texts using e-mail and mobile phones. This area of literacy practices is very different from what counts as school literacy. For a large proportion of our pupils, reading (and to a lesser extent writing) do not play a significant part in their lives out of school. It could be argued that this is even more reason why pupils should be taught to read and write well at school. Thus, it seemed appropriate in this chapter to analyse some of the links that existed between these two worlds, and to establish if the experiences of writing in the home had contributed to the children's progress at school.

Background

Much research on home–school links and literacy conducted before the introduction of the National Curriculum concentrated on younger children, and the ways parents helped them to learn to read (e.g. Davie *et al.* 1972; Wedge and Proser 1973; Newson and Newson 1977; Hannon and McNally 1986). The research evidence showed that children's reading attainment, at least as measured by reading tests, was strongly related to social class 'but it does not tell us anything about which learning experiences are critical, or why they should be critical' (Hannon 1995: 43).

There were relatively fewer research studies exploring the relationship between writing and children's later literacy development (e.g. Kroll 1983; Blatchford *et al.* 1985; Tizard *et al.* 1988; Blatchford 1991). The research on early writing experiences in the home identified a number of factors that related to later writing achievement. These factors included:

- the parents' interest in literacy;
- family reactions to one another and the outside world;
- children's handwriting at school entry;
- parents' help with writing preschool.

These findings, from a range of research studies, indicated that parents within the home context had a significant role to play in children's writing development, particularly in the early years (Weinberger 1996: 36–37). The extent to which parental involvement in their children's education at home was supported by the school was a theme in much research. For example, studies in the 1980s showed that the help that parents gave their young children often took place without the knowledge and support of the children's teachers (e.g. Tizard *et al.* 1981; Tizard and Hughes 1984; Tizard *et al.* 1988; Hall *et al.* 1989). Research with infant and nursery children showed that parents wanted to be involved in the writing education of their children, and wanted more information, though their views about the teaching of writing tended to emphasise the importance of handwriting. Furthermore, the degree of parental interest in their children's writing had 'been considerably underestimated' (Hall *et al.* 1989: 67–68).

Reviewing this earlier phase of research, Hughes commented on how parental involvement went on 'in relative isolation from the formal education system' (Hughes 1996: 101). The teachers had little idea of what parents were doing at home to help their children, and the parents' skills were not valued much by teachers, who saw themselves as the 'professionals' (Hughes 1996: 101). Analysing the evidence of research in the 1980s and 1990s, Hughes concluded that in spite of the intentions of policy makers, there had been little change in relationships between parents and schools. Though the rhetoric was about parental empowerment, 'the parents in our studies often seemed cut off from their children's schools, to lack understanding about what was happening, and to be uncertain how to express their concerns' (Hughes 1996: 108–109).

When intervention programmes took place to support literacy development in the home, they tended to focus on reading, through home–school reading schemes which targeted infant or primary school children (e.g. Hannon 1986). There was an increasing awareness, perhaps as a result of intervention programmes in the United States, that working with parents and children also meant supporting parental literacy (e.g. Brooks *et al.* 1996).

Any overview of parental involvement in the teaching of literacy revealed a large gap in the area of writing, which in developmental terms is closely linked to reading:

> Yet in terms of parental involvement practice, it [i.e. writing] has generally been ignored . . . progress in this area probably requires better analyses of pre-existing patterns of writing in families than are currently available in the research literature.
>
> (Hannon 1995: 147)

In my case study I have investigated the models of writing that were available in the home during the time that the target pupils were finishing primary school, and 'moving on up' to the secondary school. There is very little research evidence about models of writing in the home, particularly for children who are about to start at secondary school. Hannon observed that the importance of parents providing a model of literacy, particularly for older children

> goes beyond merely being seen to read and write, to a clearer demonstration of how these activities are linked to a wide range of adult purposes in the home, community and workplace.
>
> (Hannon 1995: 152)

I shall describe these sorts of links in the course of this chapter, with specific reference to writing.

Some theoretical issues

The notion of 'worlds apart', whether the literacy practices in the home and at school are part of a literacy continuum, or whether they represent different literacies, are part of a broader debate about the nature of literacy. On the one hand, there are those who argue that literacy should be regarded as a set of socially determined practices. In this view there are many different literacies, each with its own historical and ideological justifications, which are always embedded in relations of power (Street 1997: 48). At the other end of the spectrum is the cognitive, skills-based view of literacy, what Street calls the 'autonomous' model (Street 1984), which underpins much of the National Curriculum.

Street develops the idea of 'multiple literacies', which vary with time and place, and 'are embedded in specific cultural practices' (Street 1997: 50). He raises the issue of different 'literacy practices' at school and at home, particularly when a child's achievements at reading and writing are seen by the school to be problematic:

> From the school's point of view these home practices may represent simply inferior attempts at the real thing; from the researcher's point of view those home practices represent as important a part of the repertoire as different languages or language varieties.
>
> (Street 1997: 50)

The implication that all literacies are equally valid in their setting is often difficult for teachers to accept. Street's approach may be appropriate for an anthropologist who is trying to suspend his/her value judgements while conducting fieldwork, but it may not be entirely appropriate in the classroom. As MacCabe has pointed out 'the teacher tries to inculcate the values which are the very purposes of school' while at the same time 'being sensitive the values of others' (MacCabe 1998: 27). The debate between Street and MacCabe raises questions about relativism and educational values, and the differences between 'school literacy' on the one hand, and the literacy practices that take place in the home. The pluralist perspective should also make teachers rethink the importance they attach to 'school literacy'.

The fact that there could be many literacies is an unsettling one for educators, particularly those working at the boundary of home–school literacy. The teacher's business is school literacy and 'it would be self-deceiving to imagine that under current schooling arrangements all families' literacies can be accepted as a substitute for school literacy' (Hannon 2000: 35). Another problem is that the boundaries between different literacies may not be as easy to draw in practice as they are in theory (Barton and Hamilton 1998).

Hannon argued that even though there may be different literacies, they may not be *completely* different. He suggested that literacy practices should be regarded as a 'family' of social practices 'where there may be considerable overlaps and similarities between some instances' while others 'may be only distantly related. . .' (Hannon 2000: 36). He claimed that this approach enables educators to reconcile the pluralist and unitary approaches to conceptualising literacy. Opting for one approach at the expense of the other may involve a gross simplification of the processes that we are trying to understand. I shall therefore analyse the ways in which the writing activities at home were different from and also overlapped with school writing.

Where appropriate I have used Hannon's theoretical framework to describe what was important about the parents' or carers' roles in assisting the target pupils' writing development in the home. This is the ORIM model, which identifies four things that parents can provide for developing readers and writers: opportunities for learning; recognition of the child's achievements; interaction around literacy activities; and a model of literacy (Hannon 1995: 51). I have used this model where it appeared useful for the purposes of analysis.

Some methodological issues

I was not a neutral figure in any aspect of the fieldwork, and I was particularly aware of this when interviewing the parents or carers. I wrote to the families of the target pupils at the beginning of the project on school notepaper, in my role as the male Head of English at the secondary school which their children would soon be joining. I arranged the interviews over the telephone from school; all of these forms of contact emphasised my role and status.

The interviews were conducted in the afternoons or early evenings in the homes of the pupils. One of my concerns was what I should wear. Should I wear one of my 'Mr Tabor' outfits, the suit or formal jacket and tie which I wear at school, or something less formal? Perceptions of status are often linked to age and appearance. For example, Measor found that staff responded more fully to her in interviews when she dressed conservatively, as this reinforced her status as a researcher within a school (Measor 1985). The issue for me was that I was dependent on the good-will of the subjects, and I wanted to dress appropriately for the occasion. I decided to wear formal school clothes, partly because the interviews took place soon after the end of school. The interviews that I am describing here took place within the home, and there was no 'control' situation where I conducted interviews informally dressed. Thus the clothes I wore reinforced my role as Head of English at the secondary school, and this status gave me an entrée to the subjects' homes. At the same time it must have affected the way they perceived me, and the sorts of answers I received. I was a bit nervous when conducting the first interviews with Gavin's parents, and afterwards I felt that my desire to appear relaxed most probably added to the underlying tension. I was more relaxed when conducting the other interviews.

The families

The families all lived on the Windsor Estate, the oldest of the estates built in Billesley. It was developed as post-war local authority housing, and then expanded in the 1960s and 1970s to house overspill families from Birmingham. The estate also included some private housing development, and accommodated a population of about 4500. The families lived within a half-mile radius of the Fairway Junior School in council houses. Though the families lived on the same estate, within close geographical proximity to each other and the school, I was struck by the differences between the families in terms of background, employment and life-experiences. These were the four households:

- Gavin was the youngest of three siblings, and the interview with Mr and Mrs Richards took place in the front living room with Gavin present. His parents came from Carlisle, and had moved south to find work.

- Lauren lived with her grandmother and uncle. Mrs Newton (the grandmother) came originally from Birmingham, and worked as a part-time cleaner at Social Services. There were no other children in the household.

- James lived with both of his parents; Mrs Harper came from the Birmingham area, and Mr Harper was originally from Lancashire. Mrs Harper was the Senior Sister at Billesley Hospital (a community hospital), and she had also been Acting Hospital manager. Mr Harper was a ticket conductor on the local railway network. James had an elder sister who was in Year 10; she sat in on the interviews while James sat out of sight in the next room, but within earshot.

- Zoe lived with her mother, Mrs Jackson, and two younger siblings. Mrs Jackson was not working at the time of the interview; Zoe was not present when I talked to her mother. Mrs Jackson had been born and brought up in Billesley, and had attended Jeremy Priestley School.

The interviews with the parents and carers

Do you belong to a local library? Do you have a paper at home?

These questions were an 'easy' way into the interviews, but they were also important because reading and writing are connected, even though they are dealt with separately in the National Curriculum. Reading habits, and the materials the children read, often serve directly or indirectly as models of writing in addition to whatever models of writing are presented to them at school. All the households belonged to the local library, and encouraged their children to use it, or took them there. Local or national papers were read on an occasional basis; only Lauren was mentioned as reading her grandmother's paper from time to time. Both Lauren and her grandmother belonged to the local library. They went irregularly, though Mrs Newton emphasised what a keen reader Lauren was and how many books she would take out of the library. They took the *Mirror* and the *People*; Lauren picked up her grandmother's newspapers 'from time to time', and her uncle commented on how quickly she could read and understand a story in the paper.

The Richards also belonged to the local library, and took their children there every four weeks. Mr Richards tended to get a paper such as the the *Daily Express* when he was out working. James and his sister were frequent users of the public library. The parents got the *Billesley Weekly Express*, and sometimes Mrs Harper brought back a copy of the *Guardian* from work. Mrs Jackson went to the local library with her children every few weeks. Occasionally she bought the *Sun* and the *Billesley Weekly Express*.

What writing do you do as part of your job?

The writing which parents and carers did was varied and reflected their different occupations. Mr Richards was an HGV driver, and the writing he did as part of his job consisted of recording the results of his tachograph, and filling in timesheets. Mrs Richards said that she didn't do any writing for her job, which was working at the local shoe factory.

Mrs Newton (Lauren's grandmother) did no writing for her job, and Zoe's mother, when employed, did factory work. As the Senior Sister at Billesley Hospital, Mrs Harper wrote care plans and assessed managed patients 'so there's a lot of writing concerned with that'. She also wrote case notes, nursing notes, reports on junior or trainee nurses, as well as references. Mr Harper wrote (or filled in) passenger irregularity reports and accident reports when necessary, as part of his job as a ticket conductor.

What sorts of writing do you do at home?

The answers were very varied, reflecting the interests, education, professional responsibilities and roles within the home. The writing activities which the adults did in the home provided examples of writing practices that were often different from those which the children experienced at school. For example, while Mr Richards didn't do any writing at home, his wife filled in bills and wrote absence notes if Gavin was off sick.

Mrs Newton, Lauren's grandmother, had liked writing poetry since her mid-teens, and now wrote choruses for the church to which she belonged. She made up the tunes as well, usually when she was gardening or doing the housework. Other writing activities at home included lists, memos and letters. The question about writing also triggered off a discussion with her son about her good handwriting. For example, when she signed a cheque people often said, 'Oh, aren't you a lovely writer!' Thus a discussion about writing was also associated with handwriting in her mind, a point which emerged in other interviews.

Mrs Harper rarely wrote lists or memos at home, because she did so much writing at work, and preferred to use the telephone instead of writing letters. If she had to leave a message for her husband she tended to use the dictaphone. Sometimes she brought reports home that she worked on, using the word processor which was kept in the kitchen. She had just finished a four-year part-time degree in nursing at Northgrove College, which included a dissertation. Combining her degree, her job and family life had been difficult: 'obviously it affected all the family, you know. . . (when) I wasn't at work I was in the library . . .' Completing the degree had given her a tremendous feeling of achievement.

Mr Harper trained pigeons, and he kept notes on them. These notes included records of the weather, the day, the time the birds were released, how they were released and 'everything else'. He described the notes as being 'scrappy details' so that 'I know where I am', so he could see how the birds were developing. Mrs Jackson occasionally wrote letters, compiled shopping lists, and filled in forms.

The writing practices described here were not strikingly different from at least some of the writing activities which the children experienced at school, making notes or lists, writing letters or poems. Mrs Harper was unusual, compared to the other adults, in that she had completed a part-time degree and written a dissertation. These activities went on quite independently of the writing the children did at school, and were determined by a range of work, domestic and leisure factors. The main point is that the children saw at least one adult in the household doing different types of writing in the home.

Do you help your child with homework?

There were different degrees of intervention and support for the children's homework. For example, Mrs Richards said that she sometimes read over Gavin's stories, and checked spelling and punctuation, an answer which elicited a sceptical response from Mr Richards:

MR RICHARDS: Commas, do you know where to put commas and things like that, honestly, truthfully?
MRS RICHARDS: Yeah, most of the time, yeah.
MR RICHARDS: Oh good, I'll ask you next time!

Gavin usually did his homework in the front room with the rest of the family, though he went upstairs if the homework was difficult. For the Harper parents the issue was that James was set very little homework from the junior school, though I didn't find out how much he was set on a regular basis. They took an interest in what he was doing, and would ask James what his homework was. He did his homework on the floor of the sitting-room or on the dining-room table, but not in his room. James's parents tried to stop him doing homework while watching TV.

Lauren tended to do her homework downstairs in the lounge, and her grandmother helped her with 'simple' things like addressing an envelope. According to Mrs Jackson, Zoe did her homework on the floor downstairs 'half the time'. Mrs Jackson felt that Zoe had more homework to do in Year 6 compared to previous years. She didn't 'interfere' with Zoe's homework, but would read a story that Zoe had written if asked to do so.

The attitude of all the adults was supportive towards their children's homework. In general, these children were expected to get on with their homework most of the time. This was understandable, given that the adults were either in full-time employment (except Mrs Newton) or raising a young family (Mrs Jackson). In terms of writing activities in the home, the areas which the adults said they helped the children with were to correct technical and secretarial mistakes, but not (for example) to help them reshape or edit a piece of writing.

The parental input was an extra influence in correcting the children's writing, and it relied on the parents feeling confident enough to use the same (or similar) skills that the children were using at school. This confirms research conducted by Brooks *et al.* which showed that when parents had a low competence in writing, they had little confidence in their abilities to help their children improve as writers (Brooks *et al.* 1996: 32–33). Five out of the six adults I interviewed were not very confident about their writing skills, nor did they use these skills much (if at all) at work, so their attitudes to their own writing skills were similar to the findings reported by Brooks. In spite of this, they were all keen to support their children's learning where they could. Given the level of parental data, it was difficult for me to assess whether the adult writing skills present in the home made a significant difference to the performance of the target pupils at school.

What do you need to do to be a good writer?

The ambiguity of this question was useful, because it enabled me to probe what parents thought 'good writing' was. It could have referred to 'good handwriting' (which was how most of the adults interpreted it), or good at writing, in terms of mastery of different genres, which is how most English teachers would have interpreted the question. All the adults considered that handwriting, spelling and punctuation were important, to varying degrees. Content, audience and purpose, and style, all of which would concern an English teacher, were barely touched on. To some extent this may have reflected the adults' own experiences of school, and it certainly affected the things they responded to when they looked at their children's homework. One could argue that parents would quite rightly expect their children's English teachers to correct spelling, punctuation and grammar. My concern here was to identify some of the parental perceptions and priorities where 'good' writing was concerned.

For example, Mr and Mrs Richards picked out good spelling and punctuation as being important in good writing, and this led to a discussion about differences in standards between the north and the south, and the problems Gavin had with his handwriting.

Technical skills were also important for Mrs Newton, such as 'dot your Is', use full stops and apostrophes correctly – 'I never know where to put half these things' – though this lack of confidence was contrasted with Lauren's skill at using punctuation correctly. For Mrs Newton, the most important technical skills were handwriting and paragraphing, though she also thought content was important, because the topic had to be 'interesting' to justify writing about it in the first place.

Mr Harper thought that to be a good writer you would have had to have read a lot of other people's written work, so that you could get the knowledge and education of those that had gone before. This indicated an understanding of the links between writing and reading, and the fact that writers do not work in isolation from their interaction with other texts. Where technical skills were concerned, Mrs Harper thought that 'nice handwriting' and correct grammar were important, and she noticed these particularly in job applications and references. Both adults agreed that poor spelling was important in a piece of writing because it stuck out like a 'sore thumb', though their 15-year-old daughter argued that poor punctuation was more important because it 'could change the whole context. . . I mean you can take it (the meaning) in a totally different way.' Unlike the adults, their daughter was able to explain why correct punctuation was necessary for the communication of meaning.

When I asked Mrs Jackson what you needed to do to produce a good piece of writing, her initial response referred to handwriting 'evenly, do it evenly'. After much prompting from me, she said that she would respond more to a story of Zoe's if it was 'interesting', rather than if it was neatly presented (though this seemed to contradict what she had said earlier). In answer to the question which of handwriting, spelling, punctuation and grammar was the most important in a good piece of writing, Mrs Jackson commented that handwriting was the least important nowadays because so much writing was done on computers.

This led to a discussion about how she had taught her daughter to write at age three, by encouraging her to copy greetings onto a birthday card: 'I'd write something on paper, and she'd copy it onto a card.' This confirmed the findings of several research studies, which showed that about half the parents of pre-school children in the UK helped their children to learn to write (Weinberger 1996: 36). To use Hannon's ORIM model, this was one example where the parent had provided an opportunity for learning, and there had also been interaction between mother and daughter around a literacy activity.

What do you understand by standard English?

Primary and secondary teachers are expected, for example, to use grammatical knowledge to help pupils improve their writing (e.g. QCA 1999a), to understand and explain the differences between standard and non-standard forms of English (e.g. DfEE 1997b: 25) and to communicate an understanding of the structures of written and spoken English. Since the home environment has a crucial role to play in children's educational progress, it seems appropriate to investigate what knowledge the parents had about language, and I asked them what they understood by the term 'standard English'.

Mr Richards identified standard English with grammar, which he explained as meaning 'to say different words and different expressions or different words or different things'. He felt it was important that Gavin should learn to write standard English. He linked this to Gavin's habit of rushing his work, and felt that Gavin should think more about his writing and not just write things down as he was saying them. Mrs Richards didn't answer this question.

For Mrs Newton, standard English referred to 'the very basics of words, being able to string a sentence together'. She felt that it was important for Lauren to learn to use standard English because she would have it for the rest of her life, and it would help her with getting a job.

Mrs Harper initially said that she had no idea what standard English was, but in discussion commented that children were often lazy and used slang in their speech and thought that this was 'normal' grammar; she commented 'they drop the ends of their words'. In her view this accounted for their poor spelling. Mr Harper identified standard English with 'basic English', though he added that 'accent isn't very important nowadays'. I wasn't sure whether he was confusing, or at least combining, ideas about accent and dialect, and this is something that many people tend to do. Mrs Jackson said that standard English was certain 'level' of English, and after prompting from me she added that learning standard English would be important for Zoe's career.

All the adults who answered this question were thinking about English grammar and usage, and notions of correctness. I was impressed that they were prepared to answer this question at all, given that many teachers in my experience find such questions difficult. Again I was made aware of the Family Literacy Programme, which starts from the premise that most parents want to help improve their children's literacy skills, but that they can only do this if their own skills are supported and developed (e.g. Brooks *et al.* 1996). Such programmes have been successful with primary school pupils and their parents, but unsuccessful in Year 7 (Brooks *et al.* 1999: 7). By this stage pupils think it is 'uncool' to participate with their parents in literacy sessions at the secondary school.[1]

What were your experiences of learning to write at school like?

To get a fuller picture of the adults' attitudes to writing, I asked about their writing experiences at school. The ages of the adults ranged from late 30s to mid-50s, a span of almost twenty years, and this covered the change from the 11-plus secondary system (grammar schools and secondary moderns) to the comprehensive system. I wanted to know what these experiences had been like, and whether I could draw links between these experiences, and the sorts of support the adults felt able to provide for their children's writing.

The partial use of the subjects' own life histories here and in the interviews with teacher colleagues was intended to provide opportunities for the 'presentation of experience from the perspective of the subject or subjects themselves' (Hitchcock and Hughes 1995: 186). The discussion about the adults' writing experiences at school was also interesting for me as a teacher, because it made me reflect on the extent to which we do or do not make a difference to our students.

Mr Richards commented that he didn't do 'real' (joined-up?) writing until the second year of secondary school. He had no interest in school, and left without qualifications, but felt that this had not hindered him getting on in the world. Mrs Richards emphasised her

1 Personal communication, Dr Greg Brooks, August 2002.

'messy' handwriting: 'I didn't mind writing but I mean I'm not very good . . . I write small, I always have done . . .'. For both these adults, my question about their writing experiences at school was associated with the perception that their handwriting was poor.

Mrs Newton also emphasised the importance of handwriting when talking about her own experiences of school: 'most of the teachers wrote beautiful . . . they really wrote beautifully'. In fact she could not remember much about her English lessons; she did not write poems or stories at school, 'I would loved to have wrote a poem . . . I mean we weren't exactly asked to be. . . ah. . . putting our ideas down on paper or anything like that. . .' Her interest in writing poetry developed outside school, or after she had left. Mrs Newton remembered copying out of text books in different subjects, and writing the names of places on maps in geography. Mrs Newton's education had been very disrupted, because she had been in children's homes from the age of seven and sent to many different schools. As a result, she felt that she had 'missed out on a lot'.

Mrs Harper had attended a large comprehensive school in Birmingham. She had enjoyed English, and liked writing stories, but remembered being bored after studying *Romeo and Juliet* three times. An older sister had been left-handed, and at another (primary?) school had had her left hand tied behind her back to ensure that she wrote with her right hand. Mr Harper had gone to a secondary modern school in Lancashire where 'we were virtually allowed to do our own thing', and he ended up with no qualifications at the age of 15. He remembered being taught English by a Miss Gilbert, a lady in her fifties. 'I can't say she could have done me a great deal of harm because I'm not bad at English, not as such when it comes to writing things. . . I can't spell. . . I can put my punctuation in most of the right places.' However, he felt that he had learned most about how to write during his initial training in the army when he had received 'grade 3 education'. Mr Harper commented that his son James did 'joined up' writing at junior school, whereas he didn't start that till the senior school.

Mrs Jackson's experiences of English at school were not very positive, in fact she couldn't remember much about them at all. This was all the more humbling, because she had been a pupil at the Jeremy Priestley School. Mrs Jackson felt that she had not been very good at English, particularly reading, which she had found hard. 'I did like writing stories, but. . . my spelling wasn't very good.' She had also written poems, but not plays, and she had done a lot of copying out, though she could not remember what.

These recollections were a dismal commentary on many years of compulsory education. The writing experiences appeared to have been limited in range, with a lot of emphasis on handwriting, copying, and accuracy of spelling and punctuation. Five of the adults felt that they were poor at these writing skills, and only two of the adults remembered enjoying writing stories in English. These experiences may go some way to explaining the aspects of their children's writing they thought were important, and which often needed to be improved.

How should children be taught to write?

This question arose from comments made by the Harpers; it was an unplanned question which they interpreted as referring mainly to the technical skill of handwriting. Mrs Harper thought it should be made fun, that children should take more pride in their writing, and that they should practise it more, 'it's not something as far as I can see that they practise much. . .'.

This was connected with another parental concern, namely that the juniors didn't get enough homework, though Mr Harper commented that he could see his children's progress when he looked at their homework. The emphasis on handwriting was reinforced when Mrs Harper added that 'It was quite surprising at Parents' Evening this year to see how James's handwriting had improved from last year.'

Clearly both parents were looking for signs of their children's progress through the work that was brought home. Developing as a writer was identified in the first instance with improving their handwriting

What expectations do you have of the writing tasks your child will have to do as s/he moves from Year 6 to Year 7?

There was a range of views in my sample about what the writing expectations in Year 7 would be. For example, Mr Richards initially said that Gavin could only be expected to write 'to the best of his ability' in Year 7, and that he would 'advance with it', that is, make progress. He felt that Gavin still needed to improve his handwriting, but thought that at secondary school he would be writing at a 'different level'. Mrs Richards echoed this when she said that Gavin would be writing at a 'higher level' in Year 7, and that he would have to write essays and generally do 'more writing'.

Mrs Newton's expectations about Year 7 were that Lauren would have to improve on her handwriting, and that she would use computers more to help with her writing ('there's no art in it, is there?'). Mrs Harper expected that there would be a continuation, but hoped that the writing demands would be 'in more depth'. Mr Harper commented, 'I hope there'll be more demand put on James for different styles than what he's got at the moment.' Unfortunately I did not follow up what exactly Mr Harper had in mind when he talked about 'different writing styles', but he clearly had a notion of writing progression. Mrs Jackson didn't think the writing demands would be very different in Year 7 compared to the primary school, and emphasised the importance of handwriting, 'Zoe's already writing joined-up writing so to speak, so I can't see it being that different.'

For five of the six adults there was an expectation that the writing demands in Year 7 would involve more difficulty, and thus offer opportunities for progress. The adults were using their own conceptualisations of writing progression, which were expressed in terms of better handwriting; writing at a different or higher 'level'; writing essays or writing in 'more depth'; or writing in 'different styles'. The parents had not received any information from the primary or secondary schools about the writing demands of Year 7, yet these parental expectations (taken together) suggested notions of progression that in some respects were similar to, or exceeded, the expectations of the Year 7 teachers (as described in Chapter 5).

Concluding comments

In the broader context of writing at primary–secondary transition, there are certain conclusions that can be drawn from these interviews. The adults supported their children's learning where they could, and had notions of good writing and writing progression, that (to some extent) could be linked to their own experiences of writing at school. Five of the six adults did not have much confidence in their own writing skills, and this may have affected the sort of help they could offer at home. They had not received any information about writing expectations from the secondary school, though they assumed that writing in Year 7 would be more demanding than in Year 6.

All the target pupils saw examples of writing activities taking place in the home, though further research would be needed to establish how (or if) these writing activities 'influenced' the writing of the children. There appeared to be what Hannon has called 'a family resemblance' or overlap between the types of writing that took place in the home (Hannon 2000: 36), and some of the writing which the pupils did at school, for example letters, lists, cards and notes. Though these two worlds were different, they cannot be regarded as being completely apart.

Implications for the practising teacher

- The main implication for practising teachers is how we communicate our expectations about pupils' literacy (i.e. what they should be achieving) in Years 6 and 7 to parents and other carers. The parents of pupils who are about to 'move on up' from Year 6 tend to receive a lot of pastoral information that will support their child's social adjustment to the secondary school. There tends to be less communication about the literacy demands of the curriculum in Year 7, and what parents can do to help. This is a complex issue, as illustrated by the range of literacy skills possessed by the parents and carers that I interviewed. Clear communication to parents of basic literacy targets for the majority of pupils in a year group would be one step towards developing closer home–school links. For example, parents could be provided with user-friendly booklets, showing examples to illustrate the nature of the targets, and making suggestions about how parents and carers could support children in meeting them.

- This chapter also raises the issue of the impact that 'home culture' has on pupils' education, in particular their literacy development. Teachers need to strike a balance between the literacy curriculum we are required to teach, and sensitivity to the writing experiences that pupils bring into school (e.g. e-mail, text messages, Internet). These issues also raise questions about how we define writing, a point that I shall return to in the next chapter.

8   'Getting it clear': towards a critical perspective

'If seven maids with seven mops
Swept it for half a year,
Do you suppose,' the Walrus said,
'That they could get it clear?'
'I doubt it', said the Carpenter,
And shed a bitter tear.

Through the Looking Glass, Chapter 4.

Introduction

After many years of the National Curriculum, with its innumerable shifts in policy and fresh initiatives, it would be understandable if most teachers felt, at times, like the Carpenter. We can sympathise with the Walrus's question, but the Carpenter's answer shows that he is the realist. Perhaps we will never get it 'entirely clear', either in terms of understanding the complexities of government policy, or being allowed to sweep away the debris of discarded initiatives, and get on with the business of teaching and learning. Continuity and progression at primary–secondary transition continue to be problematic areas, as shown by the comments of HMCI (TES 2002a) and an official report in 2002 (OFSTED 2002a). I believe that my research suggests some reasons why this is so, and in this chapter I discuss how we might begin to think differently about our policies and practices.

This chapter is divided into three broad sections. In the first section I discuss how my main research findings about writing in Years 6 and 7 (analysed in detail in Chapters 3 to 7) contribute to our understanding of continuity, progression and transition between primary and secondary schools. The second section contains a more speculative discussion of the issues raised by my research. In the final section of the chapter I consider the implications of my findings for policy and practice, and discuss some practical suggestions about the possible ways forward.

Continuity, progression and young writers at transition

To help the reader I have summarised my main research findings in Table 8.1. The table analyses the similarities and differences in children's writing in Years 6 and 7, the pupils' perceptions of writing at transition, the expectations and approaches of their teachers where writing was concerned, and the effect of the NLS on writing at the primary–secondary interface. Where appropriate, I will refer to this table in the rest of this section.

Curriculum continuity or discontinuity?

My research indicates that there was little or no continuity between Year 6 and Year 7, if by this we mean communication between teachers about the teaching or uses of writing; this confirms much previous research. Although there were some similarities in the ways teachers taught or used writing in Year 6 and Year 7, they were not the result of joint planning or other forms of communication. These examples of unplanned continuity could be regarded as repetition in Year 6 and Year 7, but they were not instances of 'building on' what pupils had already been taught.

There was little or no communication between the primary and secondary school about expectations of the writing skills required in either phase, and this situation had not changed between 1997 and 2002. In 1997, the primary school teacher in Year 6 did not know what types of writing his pupils would be expected to do in Year 7, because he had not been told by the secondary school. The two primary teachers I interviewed in 2002 gave similar responses.

Most of the secondary teachers had little or no idea about the prior achievements of their pupils in Year 6 (Table 8.1), and information about the Key Stage 2 test results in English, mathematics and science tended to reach departments in a haphazard fashion after the start of the academic year[1]. Given the distrust many secondary teachers still feel towards Key Stage 2 assessments one can understand their desire to provide new pupils with 'the basics', to ensure that all new pupils (regardless of the primary school they had come from) were able to start the Key Stage 3 curriculum from the same knowledge and skills base.

Table 8.1 Summary of main research findings

Area of research/ research question	Main finding or issues
Were there similarities or differences in the teaching of writing in Years 6 and 7?	• Some unplanned similarities in the approaches used to teach writing in Years 6 and 7. • No communication between teachers in Years 6 and 7 about the teaching and uses of writing
Did the pupils' writing in Year 7 demonstrate progression compared to Year 6?	• Evidence of progression in the writing of argumentative essays in history in Year 7, though this was not planned continuity with Year 6. • Most of the evidence demonstrated regression in the pupils' writing in Year 7. • Pupils' existing repertoires of writing skills went largely unchallenged in Year 7. These skills were used mainly to test knowledge and understanding.
What types of writing predominated in Years 6 and 7?	• Pupils' writing limited to a few main types, though different in Years 6 and 7. • Some evidence of more copying in Year 7 than in Year 6. • Editing and redrafting in Years 6 and 7 consisted mainly of making a neat copy with corrected spelling and punctuation. • Completing a chart or a table, or labelling a figure or a graph occurred frequently in Years 6 and 7. • These writing activities are not considered significant in the research literature. This suggests that we should broaden our notion of what counts as writing.
What were the pupils' perceptions of writing in Years 6 and 7?	• They felt that there was some repetition in the types of writing they produced in Years 6 and 7. • When discussing 'good' writing they emphasised features such as spelling, punctuation and neatness in Years 6 and 7. • The types of writing they referred to most frequently were: copying, answering questions and writing stories.
How did primary and secondary teachers learn about pupils' achievements in Year 6 or Year 7?	• Most secondary school teachers had little or no idea about the prior achievements of their pupils in Year 6, including writing. • Most primary teachers in Year 6 had little idea of the writing demands their pupils would experience in Year 7. • Key Stage 2 test results and Teacher Assessments tended to reach Year 7 teachers in a haphazard manner. • Year 7 teachers tended to distrust the Key Stage 2 test results and Teacher Assessments, especially in English.

- Teachers of Year 7 pupils were unsure how to use Key Stage 2 test results to inform detailed curriculum planning.
- The Special Needs Department in the secondary school provided detailed information to Year 7 teachers about new pupils with learning difficulties.

What were the priorities for Year 7 teachers at the start of the academic year?

- Most secondary school teachers were concerned to give new pupils 'the basics' at the start of Year 7, so that all pupils would begin the Key Stage 3 curriculum with the same knowledge and skills base.
- For most secondary school teachers this was more important than liaising with teachers in Year 6.

How were expectations about the writing demands of the Year 7 curriculum communicated to teachers and pupils in Year 6, and to the parents of these pupils?

- Primary teachers, and pupils in Year 6 and their parents, had little or no idea of the writing demands of the curriculum in Year 7, i.e. what writing skills new pupils would need to be successful at the start of Key Stage 3.
- Parents would have liked to support their children's writing in Year 7, but were unsure how to do this in most cases.

Did the preparation for the Key Stage 2 tests affect curriculum delivery n Year 6?

- It appeared to distort the Year 6 curriculum, particularly in the spring term, when pupils were prepared intensively for the national tests.

How did the introduction of the NLS, and the English Framework for Teaching, at Key Stage 3 affect curriculum continuity?

- The use of starter activities, whiteboards, the lesson structure adapted from the Literacy (and Numeracy) Hours, etc. created a more interactive approach in Year 7 classrooms.
- This provided greater continuity in pupils' learning experiences between Year 6 and Year 7.

Literacy Update 2002

- The NLS at Key Stage 3 fostered whole-school approaches to the teaching of writing.
- It gave secondary school teachers additional techniques for the teaching of writing.

Additional questions

- Is the NLS embedded securely at Key Stage 3?
- What impact has it had on pupils' extended writing?
- What impact has the NLS had on teaching and learning at Key Stage 3?
- Has classroom practice really changed that much?
- Is the diet of writing activities still limited to a few main types?
- Have continuity and progression at the Key Stage 2/3 interface improved?

Other information about new pupils (both academic and pastoral) was available in the secondary school in the folders of information for each child sent by the primary schools to the Head of Year 7, but this was not in a form that was readily accessible to subject teachers. The teachers interviewed were unclear how such information (along with the results of the Key Stage 2 tests and Teacher Assessments) could or should be used to inform lesson planning, and hence promote curriculum continuity at the beginning of Year 7.

Recent research shows that attainment at 14 is the most important determinant of GCSE performance (DfEE 2001a). Thus, unless the impact of transition from primary to secondary school could be shown to have a significant impact on examination results at Key Stages 3 and 4, improving Key Stage 3 test results is more likely to be a priority for secondary schools than improving continuity and progression with their partnership primary schools.[2]

Curriculum continuity between Years 6 and 7 has been improved by the National Literacy Strategy at Key Stages 2 and 3, because it provides a common framework for the teaching of writing, and a shared language with which to discuss and share approaches to writing, though the main issue for the secondary teachers I interviewed in 2002 was the lack of time do this (Table 8.1). The use of starter activities, whiteboards, and the three- or four-fold structure of lessons in English and mathematics in particular, as well as in some other subjects, provides greater continuity for pupils in Year 7 with the approaches they are familiar with from primary school. This is particularly striking with the responses of boys, for example in the use of word and sentence activities that foster a spirit of competition or game. Pupils in Year 7 know more about language features such as similes, homophones and alliteration than they did five years ago. However, anecdotal evidence suggests that the quality of pupils' writing, particularly extended writing, is not much better than it was before the introduction of the NLS, though more research is necessary to confirm this.

Thus, the NLS has provided a greater degree of continuity between Year 6 and Year 7 in terms of shared teaching approaches, and there is more information available about the Year 6 curriculum (if only Year 7 teachers had time to evaluate it). However, as discussed above, establishing continuity in children's writing at transition is still problematic.

Developing curriculum continuity between primary and secondary teachers also becomes more difficult when there are differences in the types of discourse used. For example, the primary teacher I observed emphasised the teaching of creative writing (in preparation for the Key Stage 2 tests), and the importance of language work (spelling, punctuation, paragraphing). This conformed to the national picture; the report on the Key Stage 2 tests in 1997 (when the four target pupils took the tests) commented that more children chose to write narrative than non-narrative, and 'generally the standard of writing is higher in narrative' (QCA 1998b: 13). By contrast to the primary teacher, the Year 7 English teachers I observed placed more emphasis in their lessons on the teaching of literature, and pupils' responses to different fiction texts (see also Allen 1987; Marshall and Brindley 1998). As a result, primary and secondary teachers had different notions of what constituted 'English', and this would have made communication between the phases more difficult.

Another example of how different discourses could affect communication between primary and secondary teachers was illustrated by the ways they discussed notions of good writing. These ideas reflected a mixture of what was required by the curriculum area, as well as (in some cases) the experiences of writing of the Head of Department. As indicated in Chapter 6, the primary school teacher's notion of good writing tended to reflect an emphasis on neatness of presentation and technical accuracy. At secondary level notions of good writing in different subjects reflected a range of cognitive functions – empathetic writing in English, writing a report in science, and concise one-word answers in geography. As a result, pupils had to learn the 'ground rules' (Sheeran and Barnes 1991) for writing in different subjects at the secondary school, and this situation has not been significantly altered by the NLS.

In Chapter 7 I showed how the parents or carers of the target pupils had received little specific information about the writing demands their children would experience at the start of secondary school (Table 8.1). Most would have welcomed more information and guidance as to how they could support their children's learning at the new school, and this could contribute to continuity between primary and secondary school.

Progression or regression?

In a situation where there was little or no continuity in the teaching and uses of writing, there was also little or no progression. Most of the writing activities I observed in Year 7 classrooms in 1997/98 were based on the assumption that the pupils had acquired the necessary skills at primary school, for example writing a formal letter, setting out a newspaper or writing a science report (with the exception of writing an argumentative essay in history). For example, the writing of science reports in Year 6 showed that pupils had learned to use a formal structure in primary school, using headings provided by the teacher. However, the willingness of science teachers in the autumn term of Year 7 to accept narrative accounts of experiments suggests that there was no progression in the way reports were written, compared to Year 6.

The interview with the Head of Science in 2002 showed that, as a result of the National Literacy Strategy at Key Stage 3, a standardised approach to the writing of reports was being introduced in Years 7 to 9. As a result there was greater consistency across each year group, though more research would be required to assess the impact this had on pupils' progress in science by the end of Key Stage 3. In spite of this, there was no planned progression with the types of writing that pupils did in science at Key Stage 2.

The pupils may have been answering more difficult questions, for example in geography in the autumn term of Year 7 compared to the summer term of Year 6, but there was no evidence from the snapshot weeks of progression in their writing. Some of the most frequently occurring writing activities, such as answering questions, occurred both in Year 6 and Year 7 (Table 8.1), so there was a degree of similarity in pupils' writing experiences, but they were not developing their skills as writers. Differences in the types of writing that occurred during the snapshot week at the beginning of Year 7, compared to Year 6, may have reflected differences in the ways subjects were taught by specialist teachers at secondary school.

These findings confirm much of the research, referred to in Chapter 2, that has been conducted over the past 25 years, and which suggests that a limited range of writing activities takes place in most primary and secondary school classrooms. This also provides evidence for a more general concern that the National Curriculum has not led to an improvement of standards in either literacy or numeracy (e.g. Campbell 1996; Brooks 1998; Foxman 1998; Galton 1998). Further classroom-based research is required to investigate whether this situation has been changed significantly by the NLS at Key Stages 2 and 3.

The lack of progression described above was reflected in the target pupils' perceptions of the main writing activities at transition. They felt there was repetition in the types of writing they did at the end of Year 6, and at the beginning of Year 7. When discussing 'good' writing at the primary school and the secondary school, they emphasised features such as correct spelling and punctuation, and neatness. This suggests that the categories about writing that the pupils brought with them from primary school were not challenged or altered in Year 7. Furthermore, their perception that the primary teacher would have paid more attention to neatness and accuracy when they redrafted their stories than the secondary teacher (whether this is true or not), raises questions about what primary and secondary teachers were actually doing in the classroom when redrafting was meant to have taken place.

The different ways pupils and teachers interpret writing tasks could also affect progress. At primary school the classroom teacher has the overview of each pupil's literacy development in the class. Individual teachers in the secondary school can only deal with the literacy demands of their own subject. However, the pupils' experiences and perceptions provide the linking thread between literacy practices in and between subjects. They possess the 'underview' of how writing is taught, used and assessed across the secondary curriculum. If there is a significant disjunction between the ways pupils and teachers conceptualise writing processes, then pupils will not be doing what teachers think they should be doing, or pupils will not understand what they are meant to do, and their progress will suffer as a result. More research is required to investigate how pupils interpret and conceptualise writing tasks.

Pressures and priorities at transition

In this section I will discuss alternative models or approaches to the issues and problems raised above. I suggest ways of managing the Year 7 'dip', discuss an alternative model of progression, and consider the implications of my research for models of writing.

Managing the Year 7 'dip'

The lack of communication between primary and secondary teachers identified in this book could be regarded as one of the main causes for the Year 7 'dip'. However, it is too simplistic (and also erroneous) to say that the teachers were negligent, and to suggest that if only teachers were to do more, for example improve the transfer of information from primary to secondary schools and use it appropriately, continuity would be improved (e.g. as suggested in SCAA 1996, 1997a, 1997b; QCA 1998a). The evidence from the interview data was that teachers in both phases worked in situations of competing and often conflicting pressures, and as a result issues of cross-phase continuity had relatively low priority.

One could argue that more knowledge about (say) the teaching and uses of writing in Year 6 classrooms might enable a Year 7 teacher to avoid the repetition and replication that are conventionally held to account for the dip at the beginning of Year 7. In fact, most pupils make up the ground supposedly lost at the beginning of secondary school by the end of Year 7, and other pupils are stimulated by the 'fresh start' when they start at the new school. So is too much fuss being made about the Year 7 dip, as some secondary teachers maintain (e.g. TES 2002c)? One could argue that if the GCSE results in a school are consistently good, then it does not matter if some students appear to regress at the beginning of Year 7.

However, research shows that some pupils lose ground in Year 7 and never appear to catch up; they are in effect lost to the secondary educational system (Galton *et al.* 1999a: 11–12). The possible reasons for this are complex, and may involve a mixture of social, psychological and academic factors (*ibid.*: 12–14; 17–19). My findings identified a number of factors which could contribute to the dip in pupils' achievements at the beginning of Year 7. These included low expectations of pupils' writing skills on the part of the secondary school teachers; the absence of a shared approach across the secondary curriculum to the teaching of non-fiction genres (e.g. newspaper reports); and regression in the quality of some of the writing produced at the beginning of Year 7. The secondary teachers were not building on from the achievements of pupils in Year 6, at least not in a planned or systematic manner, because in most cases they did not know what the pupils had achieved in Year 6.

It has been suggested that one way of reducing the Year 7 dip is by the use of transition units (DfES 2002). These provide schemes of work in English and mathematics to be started at the end of Year 6, and continued at the beginning of Year 7. Though some bridging schemes have promoted closer links between primary and secondary schools (e.g. Forbes *et al.* 2002; Frater 2002), there is no convincing research evidence so far that such schemes are effective in promoting curriculum continuity.[3]

The use of transition units was intended to ensure 'greater continuity and progression and less repetition of work'. The introduction to the units acknowledged that, in spite of the Key Stage 3 Frameworks in English and mathematics, 'it is often difficult for Year 7 teachers to gauge the curricular strengths and weaknesses of pupils who are new to their schools', even if information about pupils' attainments at the end of Key Stage 2 reached the Year 7 teacher (DfES 2002: 3). Thus, the transition units were intended to provide secondary teachers with 'some common information about pupils from different primary schools' (*ibid.*: 3). The liaison and joint planning involved could be difficult if the school receives pupils from dozens of primary schools, as in some inner-city areas (Templeton and Hood 2002).

In the English materials reading and writing were linked through the use of reading logs (DfES 2002: 13). These units could give secondary English teachers something to build on, and a clearer idea of pupils' experiences at the end of Year 6. One could adapt and simplify the approach, by using the same reading logs in Years 6 and 7 for private reading. There would need to be agreement between the secondary school and the partnership schools about what types of response would be expected, so that pupils could demonstrate progression. Time for collaboration is the main constraint here, as with any cross-phase initiative.

One example of good practice was the 'Moving On Up' initiative, started in Birmingham in 1998. It consisted of a series of transition units, covering a range of subjects, but with a literacy focus (though there has also been a module in mathematics since 1999). The first version was solely English, the second covered a range of subjects, and the latest had three modules for English, history and science (revised in 2000/01). The aims of the units were to 'help pupils to look forward to secondary school in a very positive way' and to 'strengthen continuity of curriculum experience at transition' (BASS 2002: 2).

Amongst these units the latest version of the English unit, *Rites of Passage*, drew on the pupils' experiences as they moved from primary to secondary school, and gave them opportunities to reflect on the process of moving to the 'big' school. A survey was conducted by the Birmingham Advisory and Support Service in 2001 to assess this and the other units (BASS 2002). Although the survey received a low response rate, of the schools that replied about two-thirds stated that they had used the materials. A third said that they had not been able to use the materials because of pressures created through the implementation of the Key Stage 3 Strategy. Even though Heads of Department at the secondary schools said that they took notice of work sent to them by the primary schools, the majority of primary teachers felt that their secondary colleagues attached too little significance and status to this work. The potential of the modules to support Key Stage 2/3 continuity and progression was realised in only a few schools. The materials tended to be used as part of the literacy curriculum, but in general they were not being used to strengthen cross-phase links (BASS 2002: 12). The report thus highlights some of the practical problems of using transition units.

The Birmingham units were replaced in 2001/02 by the DfES transition units, and secondary schools have been encouraged to use them with support from the LEA. The initial response appears to have been positive, building on the previous three years of good practice.

A more detailed evaluation will be needed to assess the benefits of the units in promoting cross-phase continuity.[4]

These examples and my research both suggest that where schools and their teachers identify curriculum continuity as a priority, where the head teacher has a proactive approach to developing primary–secondary links, and where there is strong outside support, managing the Year 7 dip and improving progression are more likely to be effective.

A different model of curriculum continuity?

What might a different model of curriculum continuity look like? At present teachers are being presented with one paradigm by the National Literacy Strategy, that of increasing prescription in the delivery of literacy, and the way English should be taught at Key Stage 3 (DfEE 2000). The pressure to 'deliver' the English and Numeracy Frameworks leaves teachers with little time for reflection and sharing, least of all with colleagues in other schools.

I would argue that there is another paradigm. Rather than introducing more prescription, it is important for teachers to have the time to communicate, explore and learn from each other. If the baseline of the discussion is about how to raise standards, there is a strong argument for less central control of the curriculum, particularly where good schools are concerned (Campbell 1998; Dainton 1998). In that scenario primary and secondary teachers might have more opportunities for learning from each other, thereby improving continuity of the curriculum. The possibility of less control and prescription now appears to inform some recent government thinking about the curriculum (TES 2002b).

However, managing continuity and transition also suffers from two models, the curricular and the pastoral, as outlined in Chapter 2. There may be a range of reasons for this division. From a policy point of view it is easier for governments to prescribe the nature of the curriculum and the ways it should be assessed, than to consider the psycho-social factors which may affect a child's education. To manage transition successfully, both curricular and psycho-social dimensions need to be taken into account. For example, for my target pupils, adapting to the routines of the 'big' school where they were now the youngest children, with different subject teachers and more homework, was both exciting and intimidating. Their perceptions about the secondary school curriculum, and the writing tasks required by that curriculum, were only part of their experience of becoming students at the secondary school.

Research (albeit on a small scale) has also identified the social construction of gender by boys and girls as one means of developing strategies for coping with the transition to secondary school (Pratt 1999; Jackson and Warin 2000). Other research has also focused on the effects of transitions and transfers between and within schools on pupils' motivation and commitment to study (e.g. Rudduck 1996; Rudduck *et al.* 1996, Rudduck *et al.* 1997). Both the curricular and psycho-social dimensions of transition need to be taken into account when considering the effect of primary–secondary transition on pupils' achievements in Year 7.

Thus, a pupil's time in school should not be viewed only in terms of academic progress, but also in terms of the development of his/her social competence and maturity, and learning to be a 'professional pupil' (Lahelma and Gordon 1997). Even so, Galton and colleagues have pointed out that the development of extended induction programmes designed to help pupils become 'professional students' at the start of secondary school have 'so far received little attention' (Galton *et al.* 1999a: 21). This is an area that secondary schools should address if they want to improve the way pupils engage with the Key Stage 3 curriculum at the beginning of Year 7.

A further dimension to creating a new model of continuity is to build links between teachers. In Chapter 5 I suggested that teachers were neither whitings nor snails, but oysters, containing their 'pearls' of knowledge developed (mainly) through learning on the job, and the daily honing of skills in the classroom. Oysters develop their pearls in response to a piece of grit, and they do it in isolation; teachers are inevitably part of what Wenger (1998) has termed a 'community of practice'.

Wenger's approach is relevant to teachers because he argues that knowledge is socially constructed through collaboration and learning 'on the job', rather than something that exists as an autonomous body of theory in (say) a training manual. To improve transition and curriculum continuity between primary and secondary schools, we need to develop communities of 'good' practice between teachers, and provide the resources to make this possible.

How can this be achieved? Communities of good practice between schools can only be created when there is agreement about priorities and the allocation of resources. For example, in Billesley in 2002 the two secondary schools and the local tertiary college decided to work together to provide vocational GCSEs in 2002/03. There was agreement between the three heads of the institutions (and their staff) that this was important; it was in line with government policy and funds were available for this purpose. By comparison, developing links with the partnership primary schools, though recognised as worthwhile, was a relatively low priority because it would not impact directly on test results at Key Stage 3.

More creative ways have to be found to support innovation, and to share good practice within and between schools. For example, facilitated peer learning sessions could be held in schools for local clusters as twilight sessions, with some external support provided by the LEA. LEA-based websites could provide access to the good practice of other schools, thereby creating on-line communities of practice. My own experience of Heads of English Conferences (put on by the LEA) is that the informal sharing with colleagues is often the most useful part of these courses. Time made available for discussion, planning and reflection is the most valuable commodity.

Towards a new model of progression?

My research demonstrates that there is a problem with progression in writing as pupils move from Year 6 to Year 7, and I have identified a number of factors that contribute to this problem. Added to this, we should note the comments about transition in the 2002 report by HMCI on the first year of the pilot of the Key Stage 3 Strategy (OFSTED 2002b), when the Strategy was being trialled in selected schools. HMCI pointed out the 'inadequacy' of the transfer and use of information from the primary schools, and suggested that secondary schools should use this information to set targets for Year 7 pupils (e.g. OFSTED 2002b: 3, 5, 8, 18). The problems identified in the report were similar to those described in the previous documents (e.g. SCAA 1996, 1997a, 1997b; QCA 1998a). There did not seem to have been an improvement in continuity and progression in spite of the official exhortations during the intervening five or six years. The onus continues to be placed on schools to do more, and to do it better.

However, the problem with progression at primary–secondary transition is not only a matter of changing the practical arrangements between phases. If secondary teachers are so distrustful of the assessments made at the end of Key Stage 2, there might also be a problem with the way progression is conceptualised across the key stages. As discussed in Chapter 2, the fact that national test results are based on different programmes of study rather than the attainment targets means (according to Wiliam) that the test results are not comparable across the key stages (Wiliam 2001: 15). This may be one reason why the secondary teachers I interviewed did not know how to use the Key Stage 2 test results to inform their curriculum planning.

It should also be noted that discussions about progress in OFSTED reports tend to be based on the lesson observation and professional judgement of the Inspectors. There is no theoretical or conceptual framework to support or explain the conceptualisation of progress in lessons in the OFSTED reports produced by HMCI. It is unclear how general statements about progress in lessons are compatible with statements about progression between and across key stages, based on national tests, when there is no conceptual framework to explain how these two bodies of data are related. Furthermore, I would argue that the notion of progression enshrined in the National Curriculum levels for English is restrictive, because it focuses mainly on notions of linguistic correctness, to the detriment of our pupils' development as creative writers.

What then would an alternative model of progression in writing look like? If the programmes of study at the different key stages were abolished, and the attainment targets were expanded so that each was like a mini-syllabus, the level (or levels) assigned to each pupils at a particular point in his/her education would give much clearer information about that pupils' achievements, rather than referring to different programmes of study, as at present. In other words, the information based on these expanded levels would give a more reliable picture of a pupil's progress through primary and secondary school. This model is similar to that used in the Scottish National Curriculum (SOED 1991) where the teaching and learning of English are presented in terms of 4 broad 'attainment outcomes': listening, talking, reading and writing. Progression is provided by dividing each attainment outcome into five main levels (A–E), and there is a programme of study for each level. The crucial difference with the English system is that the levels are not linked to age-related programmes of study for each key stage[5].

If tests were used there could be a common set of tiered papers for Key Stages 2 and 3, rather than different papers for each key stage (Wiliam 2001: 18). The information passed to teachers at the next key stage 'would provide clear evidence of where the students were in their learning' (*ibid.*: 18), and progression across the primary–secondary divide would be easier to establish.

Once we agree that progression is about 'getting better', we have to decide what getting better in writing means, that is, what each level would look like. This is bound to be a contentious issue among English teachers, though there is much best practice that could be drawn on. In an alternative framework for progression in writing each level could consist of (say) several main areas or strands focusing on key skills (see list below). Most pupils might make more progress in one area or strand than another, though the teacher could build up a composite picture of which level a pupil had achieved.

As shown by my research, secondary teachers in specific subject areas (and to a lesser extent the primary teacher) tend to emphasise different aspects of writing, depending on the cognitive demands of the subject. The list below summarises many of these concerns:

- writing for thinking and learning
- writing for communication
- writing for meaning, imagination, empathy
- writing to test knowledge
- the linking of audience, purpose and form in writing
- accuracy in writing: spelling, punctuation and grammar
- sensitivity to vocabulary and structure in the planning of writing
- the development of skills such as editing and redrafting, and note taking
- the use of ICT in writing
- exploring links between writing and reading, and between writing and speaking and listening (to include drama)

Turning each level into a mini-syllabus would not be easy, but tentative agreement between teachers and policy makers about the content of each level should be possible. The revised framework needs to take into account the ways pupils would understand what 'getting better' at writing means. If the new model is primarily intended to support pupils' learning, then thought has to be given as to how the notion of progression is shared with the pupils, for example through user-friendly booklets and 'can do' posters prominently displayed in classrooms.

Another problem with an all-embracing framework is that the excitement of learning (and teaching) gets swamped by the checklist of things that have to be covered. I would rename attainment targets 'discovery targets', not as a cynical exercise in re-branding, but as a means of making the pupils' learning the focus of classroom practice, rather than placing the emphasis on summative assessment through the use of end-of-key stage tests.

This section has been somewhat speculative, but these ideas have grown out of my research and my own experiences of teaching, and could contribute to the improvement of continuity and progression in writing between Key Stages 2 and 3.

Models of writing

My research challenges assumptions about the nature of writing in primary and secondary schools, particularly where genre theory is concerned. What the genre theorists ignore, by and large, are the ways the teaching and uses of writing are situated within the broader context of curriculum delivery in primary and secondary classrooms. My findings show that a significant proportion of pupils' writing in Year 6 and Year 7 consisted of filling in tables and completing charts. Though these activities have not been commented on in the research literature, possibly because these activities were not regarded as types of writing, my data suggest that we need to widen our notions of what counts as literacy. The notion of literacy has been broadened to include new forms such as on-screen literacy and moving-image media (e.g. Kress 1996; Kress and van Leeuwen 1996; Andrews 2000). Completing charts or tables, and labelling figures or diagrams are also part of pupils' literacy experiences in school. Thus I would argue that we need to broaden our notion of what counts as writing.

In practice, and especially where the teaching of English is concerned, the notion of progression described in the National Curriculum Orders (DfE 1995a; DfEE/QCA 1999) is a linguistic model, based on notions of the formal organisation of types or genres of writing. As D'Arcy (2000) has pointed out, this model has been used in the setting and marking of national tests at Key Stages 2 and 3.

Writing for meaning, learning and communication has been subordinated to this predominantly linguistic model of correctness. This linguistic model determines how pupils are taught writing, and how their writing is assessed, and it also affects how pupils are prepared for national tests. As a result, 'They may do better in the tests for which they have been prepared, putting in all the full stops and writing in paragraphs, but they are unlikely to be activated into that "mutual dependence of language and thought". . .' (D'Arcy 2000: 51) that links writing to the creation of meaning. D'Arcy argues that writing is a mental process that generates thinking, and the communication of thought and feeling. She further argues that this process-based approach to writing offers an alternative paradigm to the linguistic approach, although she suggests that both approaches should be complementary (D'Arcy 2000: 51).

My research supports D'Arcy's view. Secondary teachers of history and English in particular are not limited to either the model of linguistic correctness or the 'process' model. In the classroom they emphasised different aspects of these models (without consciously identifying them as such), depending on the task that pupils were presented with. Thus, these two models do not have to be mutually exclusive, though for policy makers to accept this might mean placing more trust in teacher assessment than occurs at present.

Recent research has also called into question the theoretical rationale behind the National Literacy Strategy. It has been argued that there is insufficient evidence to support the Framework for Teaching in English, with its emphasis (for example) on short-term lesson objectives, and the dominance of grammar teaching objectives for writing (Wyse 2002: 13). It may be that a more critical evaluation of the pedagogy of the Framework is required 'to support a closer match between evidence, teaching and learning' (Wyse 2002: 13).[6]

Implications for policy and practice

I am now drawing this particular story to a close, but unlike the King of Hearts I know that the issues raised in this book are on-going; they do not stop at the last page. I hope that I have given the reader new ways of thinking about continuity, progression and transition, and I have also raised questions about what counts as writing. The following implications for policy and practice may provide some signposts for the way ahead.

Policy

1. Official exhortations and policy documents will not be enough to make curriculum continuity happen between primary and secondary schools. Curriculum continuity has to be a priority, not just within a cluster of schools, but within an LEA. The development and use of transition units could enhance continuity and progression between primary and secondary schools, but the Birmingham experience suggests that teachers and schools need support from the LEA to make this work. Creating communities of practice between primary and secondary schools would benefit teachers and pupils, by focusing (for example) on issues of pedagogy and assessment.
2. My research into writing, and the research of others on the broader issues of assessment, suggest that there is a problem with the way progression is conceptualised in the National Curriculum. This becomes particularly apparent when considering the difficulties teachers have with using levels across Key Stages 2 and 3. Policy makers need to review the construction of progression, and the relationship between the attainment targets and the programmes

of study. However, this is a 'high risk' proposal, because if followed through it could undermine the validity of the comparisons that are made between the national tests at Key Stages 2 and 3. On the other hand, failure to review this area will mean that the difficulties teachers experience in interpreting and using Key Stage 2 assessments at the start of Year 7 (as described in this book) will continue, and the progression of some pupils at secondary school will be affected.

3. My research suggests that teachers are under pressure to emphasise (either implicitly or explicitly) a model of writing based on notions of linguistic correctness. This is not true all the time, nor in all cases, but this model appears to determine to a considerable extent the ways (for example) writing is marked in the national tests at the end of Key Stages 2 and 3. The national tests have, in effect, become the model for English, particularly at primary school. My research suggests that the teaching of writing for the creation of meaning, and the development of thought and communication, is downgraded as a result. Combining a more process-based approach with the model of linguistic correctness could contribute to an improvement in pupils' writing. Finding ways of motivating pupils so that they want to write, through (for example) collaborative writing, cross-curricular projects, working with writers and poets and the use of ICT, is no less important than using writing frames or the whole-class teaching of grammar (where and when it is appropriate).

4. More research is required into how pupils conceptualise writing tasks, and the ways they construct progression in writing. At secondary school the pupils have what I have termed the 'underview' of writing (and other literacy practices) across the curriculum. If there is a significant disjunction between the pupils' constructions of what writing tasks involve, and those of their teachers, the pupils' progress will suffer.

5. I have suggested that labelling, and completing charts, figures and tables form a significant part of pupils' writing in Years 6 and 7. Research is required to establish whether this is true in other schools. If it is, we need to broaden our notion of what counts as writing.

6. Recent research suggests that some primary teachers still stick rigidly to the structure of the Literacy Hour, at the expense of allowing pupils to develop their questioning and reasoning skills (Hardman *et al.* 2002). However, many primary teachers have reacted against the over-prescriptive curriculum, and have launched

a campaign through the TES to bring creativity back into the classroom (Brighouse 2003; Hofkins 2003). Teachers should retain confidence in their experience and judgement, which are developed and refined on a daily basis in the classroom, and not allow themselves to feel deskilled by the latest directive. Primary and secondary schools should also be encouraged to set their own targets for the end-of-key stage tests.

7. My research has described and analysed the equivalent of what Jane Austen called her 'two inches wide' of ivory,[7] yet the over-riding message to the Secretary of State for Education from the teachers I interviewed would, I think, be the same in most schools in England. The message is: to do a good job we need less prescription, less testing, fewer new initiatives, more trust in teachers' professionalism and judgements, and more time for reflection, sharing and building communities of good practice.

Practice

Improvements in practice will usually be successful if one takes small steps, and builds on existing good practice. I would refer you to the list at the end of Chapter 7 on how to improve the teaching and learning of writing. My approach owes a lot to the work of Lewis and Wray,[8] and to the approaches used in the English Department at my school, and other local schools. These suggestions are not particularly original, but they work, and they can act as a stimulus to improving practice. In addition

1. The communication of expectations should be improved between primary and secondary schools, and between secondary schools and the parents of new pupils. Primary teachers, pupils in Year 6, and their parents would be helped if they knew what writing skills were needed to be successful in Year 7. (This could be extended to include the other core literacy and numeracy skills.) Teachers of Year 6 pupils could alter their teaching after the Key Stage 2 tests in the light of this information, thereby helping pupils to prepare more effectively for the transfer to the secondary school.

2. Parents could be advised on how they can support the development of their child's literacy skills at the beginning of secondary school. This sounds easy, though in practice it is not, and in Chapter 7 I described some of the difficulties involved in asking parents to support their children's skills as writers. This is an area worth

exploring, using best practice from other schools and national agencies. Finding the time to do this is another issue.

3. The Year 7 dip could be reduced if there was a whole-school cross-curricular induction programme at the start of Year 7, in which pupils were given literacy training to develop and reinforce the skills they would need. For example, note taking, editing and redrafting, skimming and scanning texts, use of the library, team building through shared activities, as well as giving them the confidence to start their careers as 'professional students' at secondary school. Such a programme would have to be dynamic, interactive and challenging, and could draw on the best practice from other schools. Older pupils could act as buddies, as happens in many schools, and mentor the new pupils, or help them develop particular skills.

4. Curriculum continuity between primary and secondary schools could be improved by the use of transition units, but only if they are kept simple, and if there is adequate time for the teachers involved to plan together.

5. The structure of lessons provided by the Literacy (and Numeracy) Strategies has given pupils some continuity in their experience of teaching styles as they start Year 7, though my impression is that these changes are not yet embedded at Key Stage 3. If the National Literacy and Numeracy Strategies, and the English Framework at Key Stage 3 are making secondary school teachers think more about the objectives and pace of lessons, then teaching and learning will improve. However, unless there are more fundamental changes in national policy, many of the problems of continuity and progression between primary and secondary schools identified in this book are likely to persist.

Notes

1 This has changed in 2002/03, with a standardised approach to the electronic transfer of test results from primary to secondary schools. This does not affect my basic argument about the usefulness of the information, or the ways it can be used by the teachers of Year 7 classes.

2 Recent research (Smith 2002) suggests that socio-economic factors are more reliable indicators of underachievement than scores in national or CATs tests, though more research is required to confirm this.

3 The Nottinghamshire LEA website www.twiyo.net contains a detailed account of the DfES transition units for Years 6 and 7 in English. I am grateful to Claire Frecknall (NIAS) for drawing my attention to this website. In science, a booklet called *Bubbles*, designed by Cheshire teachers, has proved very successful, and has been taken up by other LEAs (Hargreaves and Galton 2002: 195).

4 I am grateful to Dr P. Manford (BASS) for providing information about the Birmingham initiative, and for her comments on earlier drafts of this section.

5 There are problems of regression or hiatuses in pupils' progress when they move from primary to secondary school in Scotland, which suggest that these problems have deep-seated roots in the institutional structures of schools and schooling (personal communication, Sheila Hughes, October 2002). This should not detract from my argument that the conceptualisation of progression in writing in the English National Curriculum is deeply flawed.

6 See also Wyse 2000; Wyse 2001; Wyse and Jones 2001, for further critiques of the NLS.

7 Jane Austin, *Letter*, 16 December 1816.

8 For example, Lewis and Wray 1995, 1998, 2000.

Bibliography

Allen, D. (1987) *Teaching English since 1965: How much growth?* London, Heinemann.

Andrews, R. (2000) 'Learning, literacy and ICT: what's the connection?' *English in Education*, 34(3): 3–18.

Applebee, A.N. (1978) *The Child's Concept of Story*, Chicago, University of Chicago Press.

Barrs, M. (1994) 'Genre theory: what's it all about?' in Stierer, B. and Maybin, J. (eds), *Language, Literacy and Learning in Educational Practice*, Clevedon, Multilingual Matters with the Open University, pp. 248–257.

Barton, D. (1994) *Literacy*, Oxford, Blackwell.

Barton, D. and Hamilton, M. (1998) *Local Literacies: Reading and Writing in One Community*, London, Routledge.

Beard, R. (1984) *Children's Writing in the Primary School*, London, Hodder & Stoughton.

Beard, R. (1987) 'Parents and the writing process', in Smith, P. (ed.) *Parents and Teachers Together*, London, Macmillan Education, pp. 165–174.

Bereiter, C. and Scardamalia, M. (1987) *The Psychology of Written Composition*, Hillsdale, New Jersey, Lawrence Erlbaum Associates.

Birmingham Advisory Support Service (2002) 'Moving on up', Birmingham, Birmingham City Council, Education Department.

Black, P.J. (1998) 'Curriculum goals and improved learning', in Dainton, S. (ed.), *Take Care, Mr. Blunkett*, London, Association of Teachers and Lecturers, pp. 74–75.

Blatchford, P. (1991) 'Children's writing at seven years: associations with handwriting in school entry and preschool factors', *British Journal of Educational Psychology*, 61: 73–84.

Blatchford, P., Burke, J., Farquhar, C., Plewis, I. and Tizard, B. (1985) 'Educational achievement in the infant school: the influence of ethnic origin, gender and home on entry skills', *Educational Research*, 27(1): 52–60.

Blunkett, D. (2000) *Raising Aspirations in the 21st Century*, London, DfEE.

Board of Education (1927) *Report of the Consultative Committee on the Education of the Adolescent* (The Hadow Report), London, HMSO.

Brighouse, T. (2003) 'Suffocated by Victorian values', in *The Times Educational Supplement*, 2 May, p. 21.

Britton, J., Burgess, T., Martin, N., McLeod, A. and Rosen, H. (1975) *The Development of Writing Abilities (11–16)*, London, Macmillan.

Brooks, G. (1998) 'Trends in standards of literacy in the United Kingdom, 1948–1996', *Topic*, 19(1): 1–10.

Brooks, G., Gorman, T., Harman, J., Hutchinson, D. and Wilkin, A. (1996) *Family Literacy Works*, London, Basic Skills Agency.

Brooks, G., Harman, J., Hutchinson, D., Kendall, S. and Wilkin, A. (1999) *Family Literacy for New Groups*, London, Basic Skills Agency.

Brown, B., Taggart, B., McCullum, B. and Gipps, C. (1996) 'The impact of Key Stage 2 tests', *Education 3–13*, 24(3): 3–7.

Burtis, P., Scardamalia, M., Bereiter, C. and Tetroe, J. (1983) 'The development of planning in writing', in Kroll, B. and Wells, G. (eds) *Explorations in the Development of Writing*, London, Wiley, pp. 153–174.

Campbell, R.J. (1996) *Standards of Literacy and Numeracy in English Primary Schools: A Real or Manufactured Crisis?* University of Warwick, CREPE.

Campbell, R.J. (1998) 'Broader thinking about the primary school curriculum', in Dainton, S. (ed.) *Take Care, Mr. Blunkett*, London, Association of Teachers and Lecturers, pp. 96–101.

Campbell, R.J. and Kyriakides, L. (2000) 'Pedagogy, performance, and politics: issues in the study of primary education', *Teaching and Teacher Education*, 16: 269–273.

Castle, J. and Lawrence, I. (eds) (1987) *Continuity Models in the Curriculum: A Handbook for Teachers*, London, West London Press.

Chomsky, N. (1965) *Aspects of a Theory of Syntax*, Cambridge MA, Massachusetts University Press.

Christie, F. (1984) *Children's Writing: Study Guide*, Geelong, Deakin University Press.

Collerson, J. (ed.) (1988) *Writing for Life*, Rozelle, NSW., Primary English Teaching Association.

Cox, B. (1995) *Cox on the Battle for the English Curriculum*, London, Hodder & Stoughton.

Cumberland-Harper, J. (1991) 'Pastoral liaison at Daventry William Parker School', in Tabor, D.C., *Curriculum Continuity in English and the National Curriculum*, London, Falmer Press, pp. 11–17.

Cutler, V. (1984) 'Liaison between primary and secondary school', *Secondary Education Journal*, 14(1): 7–8.

Czerniewska, P. (1992) *Learning about Writing*, Oxford, Blackwell.

Dainton, S. (1998) 'Introduction', in Dainton, S. (ed.), *Take Care, Mr. Blunkett*, London, Association of Teachers and Lecturers, pp. 13–15.

D'Arcy, P. (2000) *Two Contrasting Paradigms for the Teaching and the Assessment of Writing*, Sheffield, NATE (with NAAE and NAPE).

Davie, R., Butler, N. and Goldstein, N. (1972) *From Birth to Seven: A Report of the National Child Development Study*, London, Longman/National Children's Bureau.

Delamont, S. (1983) 'The ethnography of transfer', in Galton, M. and Willcocks, J. (eds), *Moving from the Primary Classroom*, London, Routledge, Kegan and Paul, pp. 95–154.

Delamont, S. and Galton, M. (1986) *Inside the Primary Classroom*, London, Routledge and Kegan Paul.

Department for Education (DfE) (1995a) *English in the National Curriculum*, London, HMSO.

Department for Education (1995b) *Mathematics in the National Curriculum*, London, HMSO.

Department for Education (1995c) *Science in the National Curriculum*, London, HMSO.

Department for Education (1995d) *History and the National Curriculum*, London, HMSO.

Department for Education (1995e) *Geography in the National Curriculum*, London, HMSO.

Department for Education and Employment (DfEE) (1996) *Review of Assessment and Testing Consultation Paper*, London, DfEE.

Department for Education and Employment (1997a) *The Implementation of the National Literacy Strategy*, London, DfEE.

Department for Education and Employment (1997b) *Teaching: High Stakes, High Standards*, London, Teacher Training Agency.

Department for Education and Employment (1999a) *The National Literacy Strategy: Key Stage 3 Literacy Conferences*, London, DfEE.

Department for Education and Employment (1999b) *The National Literacy Strategy: An Interim Evaluation*, London, DfEE.

Department for Education and Employment (2000) *The National Literacy Strategy. Transforming Key Stage 3: National Pilot English at Key Stage 3*, London, DfEE.

Department for Education and Employment (2001a) *The National Strategy for Key Stage 3 (OHTs)*, London, DfEE.

Department for Education and Employment (2001b) *Key Stage 3 National Strategy, Framework for Teaching English: Years 7, 8 and 9*, London, DfEE.

Department for Education and Employment/Qualifications and Curriculum Authority (1999) *English, the National Curriculum for England*, DfEE/QCA.

Department for Education and Skills (DfES) (2002) *The Literacy, Numeracy and Key Stage 3 National Strategies. Transition from Year 6 to Year 7 English. Units of Work*, London, DfES.

Department of Education and Science (DES) (1967) *Children and their Primary Schools* (The Plowden Report), London, HMSO.

Department of Education and Science (1975) *A Language for Life* (Bullock Report), London, HMSO.

Department of Education and Science (1982) *Mathematics Counts* (The Cockcroft Report), London, HMSO.

Department of Education and Science (1989) *Education Observed 10: Curriculum Continuity at 11-plus*, London, HMSO.

Department of Education and Science/Welsh Office (1989) *English in the National Curriculum*, London, HMSO.

Department of Education and Science/Welsh Office (1990) *English in the National Curriculum (No. 2)*, London, HMSO.

Derricott, R. (ed.) (1985) *Curriculum Continuity: Primary to Secondary*, Windsor, NFER-Nelson.

Devo, J. (2003) 'Tough but tender', *Teaching Today*, 37: 24–25.

Dixon, R.T. (1985) 'Linking primary and secondary schools through a language and learning group', *Education 3–13*, 13(1): 29–31.

Doddington, C., Flutter, J. and Rudduck, J. (1999) 'Exploring and explaining "dips" in motivation and performance in primary and secondary schooling', *Research in Education*, 61: 29–38.

Dodds, P. and Lawrence, I. (eds) (1984) *Curriculum Continuity: Fact or Fiction?* London, Education Department of the West London Institute of Higher Education.

Doherty, P. (1984) 'Moving on', *Junior Education*, 8(6): 13.

Doyle, L. and Herrington, N. (1998) 'Bridging the gap: a case study of curriculum continuity at Key Stage 2/Key Stage 3 transfer', *Management in Education*, 12(3): 11–13.

Findlay, F.D. (1983) 'Continuity and liaison in language', *Education 3–13*, 11(1): 21–24.

Findlay, F.D. (1987) 'A primary/secondary joint project', in Findlay, F.D. (ed.), *Moving On: Continuity and Liaison in Action*, Sheffield, NATE, pp. 41–43.

Forbes, S., Green, R., Sparrow, G. and Wakefield, J. (2002) 'Bridging the gap', *Literacy Today*, 31: 11–12.

Foxman, D. (1998) 'Monitoring trends in numeracy in the United Kingdom, 1953–1995', *Topic*, 19(2): 1–10.

Frater, G. (2002) *Bridges for Literacy*, London, Basic Skills Agency.

Galton, M. (1998) 'Reliving the Oracle experience: back to basics or back to the future?', University of Warwick, CREPE.

Galton, M. and Willcocks, J. (1983) *Moving From the Primary Classroom*, London, Routledge, Kegan and Paul.

Galton, M., Gray, J. and Rudduck, J. (1999a) *The Impact of School Transition and Transfers on Pupil Progress and Attainment*, London, DfEE.

Galton, M., Hargreaves, L., Comber, C., Wall, D. and Pell, A. (1999b) *Inside the Primary Classroom: 20 Years On*, London, Routledge.

Galton, M., Simon, B. and Croll, P. (1980) *Inside the Primary Classroom*, London, Routledge and Kegan Paul.

Garton, A. and Pratt, C. (1989) *Learning to be Literate*, Oxford, Blackwell.

Geertz, C. (1973) *The Interpretation of Cultures*, New York, Basic Books.

Gilbert, P. (1994) 'Authorizing disadvantage: authorship and creativity in the language classroom', in Stierer, B. and Maybin, J. (eds), *Language, Literacy and Learning in Educational Practice*, Clevedon, Multilingual Matters with the Open University, pp. 258–276.

Gorman, T. and Brooks, G. (1996) *Assessing Young Children's Writing*, London, Basic Skills Agency.

Gorwood, B.T. (1986) *School Transfer and Curriculum Continuity*, London, Croom Helm.

Graves, D. (1983) *Writing: Teachers and Children at Work*, Portsmouth, New Hampshire, Heinemann.

Guardian Education (2000) 'Changing places', 22 February, pp. 2–3.

Gubb, J., Gorman, T. and Price, E. (1987) *The Study of Written Composition in England and Wales*, Windsor, NFER-Nelson.

Hall, N., Herring, G., Henn, H. and Crawford, L. (1989) *Parental Views on Writing and the Teaching of Writing*, Manchester, School of Education, Manchester Polytechnic.

Hannon, P. (1986) 'Teachers' and parents' expectations of parental involvement in the teaching of reading', *Cambridge Journal of Education*, 16(1): 28–37.

Hannon, P. (1995) *Literacy, Home and School*, London, Falmer Press.

Hannon, P. (2000) *Reflecting on Literacy in Education*, London, RoutledgeFalmer.

Hannon, P. and McNally, J. (1986) 'Children's understanding and cultural factors in reading test performance', *Educational Review*, 38(3): 269–280.

Hardman, F., Smith, F. and Wall, K. (2003) 'Interactive whole class teaching in the National Literacy Strategy', *Cambridge Journal of Education*, 33(2): 197–215.

Hargreaves, L. and Galton, M. (2002) *Transfer From the Primary Classroom, Twenty Years on*, London, RoutledgeFalmer.

Harpin, W. (1976) *The Second 'R': Writing Development in the Junior School*, London, Allen and Unwin.

Harris, S. and Rudduck, J. (1993) 'Establishing the seriousness of learning in the early years of secondary schooling', *British Journal of Educational Psychology*, 63(2): 322–336.

Henderson, E.H. (1981) *Learning to Read and Spell: The Child's Knowledge of Words*, DeKlab, Illinois, Northern Illinois University Press.

Her Majesty's Inspectorate (1993) *Boys and English: A Report from the Office of Her Majesty's Chief Inspector for Schools*, London, HMSO.

Herrington, N. and Doyle, L. (1997) *Curriculum Continuity Between Primary and Secondary School*, London, Teacher Training Agency.

Hofkins, H. (2003) 'Free their minds', *The Times Educational Supplement*, 2 May, p. 20.

Huggins, M. and Knight, P. (1997) 'Curriculum continuity and transfer from primary to secondary school: the case of history', *Educational Studies*, 23(3): 333–348.

Hughes, M. (1995) 'Introduction', in Hughes, M. (ed.) *Progression in Learning*, Clevedon, Multilingual Matters, pp. 1–14.

Hughes, M. (1996) 'Parents, teachers and schools', in Bernstein, B. and Brennan, J. (eds), *Children, Research and Policy*, London, Falmer Press, pp. 96–110.

Jackson, C. and Warin, J. (2000) 'The importance of gender as an aspect of identity at key transition points in compulsory education', *British Educational Research Journal*, 26(3): 375–391.

Jarman, R. (1993) 'Real experiments with bunsen burners', *School Science Review*, 74(268): 19–29.

Jarman, R. (1997) 'Fine in theory', *Educational Research*, 39(3): 291–310.

Jennings, K. and Hargreaves, D.J. (1981) 'Children's attitudes to secondary school transfer', *Educational Studies*, 7(1): 35–39.

Jones, I., Rose, T. and Tabor, D.C. (1996) 'Learning from the past', *Teaching History*, 83: 17–18.

Jones, L. (1995) 'Continuity in the curriculum', *Forum*, 37(2): 44–45.

Kress, G. (1982) *Learning to Write*, London, Routledge.

Kress, G. (1996) *Before Writing. Rethinking the Paths to Literacy*, London, Routledge.

Kress, G. and van Leeuwen, T. (1996) *Reading Images: The Grammar of Visual Design*, London, Routledge.

Kroll, B.M. (1981) 'Developmental relationships between speaking and writing', in Kroll, B.M. and Vann, R.J. (eds), *Exploring Speaking–Writing Relationships: Connections and Contrasts*, Urbana, Illinois, National Council of Teachers of English, pp. 32–54.

Kroll, B.M. (1983) 'Antecedents of individual differences in children's writing attainment', in Kroll, B.M. and Wells, G. (eds), *Explorations in the Development of Writing*, Chichester, Wiley.

Lahelma, E. and Gordon, T. (1997) 'First day in secondary school; learning to be a "professional pupil"', *Educational Research and Evaluation*, 3(2): 119–139.

Lance, A. (1994) 'The case for continuity', *Forum*, 36(2): 46–47.

Lance, A. (1995) 'Transferring to secondary schools: whose choice?', *Forum*, 37(2): 46–47.

Langer, E.J. (1986) 'Reading, writing and understanding: an analysis of the construction of meaning', *Written Communication*, 3: 219–267.

Lee, B., Harris, S. and Dickinson, P. (1995) *Continuity and Progression 11–16: Developments in Schools*, Slough, NFER.

Lewis, M. and Wray, D. (1995) *Developing Children's Non-Fiction Writing*, Leamington Spa, Scholastic.

Lewis, M. and Wray, D. (1998) *Writing Across the Curriculum: Frames to Support Learning*, University of Reading, Reading and Language Information Centre.

Lewis, M. and Wray, D. (2000) *Literacy in the Secondary School*, London, Fulton.

Lunzer, E. and Gardner, K. (1979) *The Effective Use of Reading*, London, Heinemann for the Schools Council.

MacCabe, C. (1998) 'A response to Brian Street', *English in Education*, 32(1): 26–28.

Marshall, B. and Brindley, S. (1998) 'Cross-phase or just lack of communication:

models of English at Key Stages 2 and 3 and their possible effect on pupil transfer', *Changing English*, 5(2): 123–133.

Martin, J.R. (1985) *Factual Writing: Exploring and Challenging Social Reality*, Oxford, Oxford University Press.

Martin, N. (1977) 'Writing', in Marland, M. (ed.), *Language Across the Curriculum*, London, Heinemann, pp. 145–168.

Martin, N., D'Arcy, P., Newton, B. and Parker, R. (1976) *Writing and Learning Across the Curriculum 11–16*, London, Ward Lock Educational.

Measor, L. (1985) 'Interviewing; a strategy in qualitative research', in Burgess, R.G. (ed.), *Strategies of Educational Research: Qualitative Method*, Lewis, Falmer Press.

Medwell, J.A. (1998) *The Context of Children's Writing in Junior Classes*, PhD thesis, Faculty of Education, University of Exeter.

Millard, E. (1997) *Differently Literate: Boys, Girls and the Schooling of Literacy*, London, Falmer Press.

Minnis, M., Seymour, K. and Schagen, I. (1998) *National Results of Years 3, 4 and 5 Optional Tests*, Slough, NFER.

National Writing Project (1989a) *Becoming a Writer*, Walton-on-Thames, Nelson.

National Writing Project (1989b) *Writing and Learning*, Walton-on-Thames, Nelson.

National Writing Project (1989c) *Audiences for Writing*, Walton-on-Thames, Nelson.

National Writing Project (1989d) *Responding to and Assessing Writing*, Walton-on-Thames, Nelson.

National Writing Project (1990a) *Ways of Looking*, Walton-on-Thames, Nelson.

National Writing Project (1990b) *Perceptions of Writing*, Walton-on-Thames, Nelson.

National Writing Project (1990c) *A Rich Resource: Writing and Language Diversity*, Walton-on-Thames, Nelson.

National Writing Project (1990d) *Writing Partnerships (1): Home, School and Community*, Walton-on-Thames, Nelson.

National Writing Project (1991) *Changing Practice: a History of the National Writing Project 1985–1989*, York, National Curriculum Council.

Naylor, J. (1990) 'Across the great divide: an experiment in liaison', *Education 3–13*, 18(2) 55–59.

Newson, J. and Newson, E. (1977) *Perspectives on School at Seven Years Old*, London, Allen and Unwin.

Nicholls, G. and Gardner, J. (1999) *Pupils in Transition*, London, Routledge.

Nisbet, J. and Entwistle, N.J. (1969) *The Transition to Secondary Education*, London, University of London Press.

Office for Standards in Education (OFSTED) (1993) *Boys and English*, London, OFSTED.

Office for Standards in Education (1998) *The Annual Report of her Majesty's Chief Inspector of Schools 1996/97*, London, The Stationery Office.

Office for Standards in Education (1999a) *The Annual Report of Her Majesty's Chief Inspector of Schools 1997/98*, London, The Stationery Office.

Office for Standards in Education (1999b) *The National Literacy Strategy, An Interim Evaluation*, HMI Report 179, London, OFSTED.

Office for Standards in Education (2001) *The Annual Report of Her Majesty's Chief Inspector of Schools 2000*, London, The Stationery Office.

Office for Standards in Education (2002a) *Changing Schools: An Evaluation of the Effectiveness of Transfer Arrangements at Age 11*, London, Office for Standards in Education/HMI Report 550, www.ofsted.gov.uk.

Office for Standards in Education (2002b) *The Key Stage 3 Strategy: Evaluation of the First Year of the Pilot*, London, Office for Standards in Education.

Perera, K. (1984) *Children's Writing and Reading*, Oxford, Blackwell.

Piaget, J. (1926) *The Language and Thought of the Child*, Florida, Harcourt Brace Jovanovich.

Pollit, A. (1999) *The Key Stage 3 Dip*, London, QCA.

Pratt, S.D. (1999) 'Movin' on up: a case study of boys transferring to secondary school from one primary school', paper presented at the BERA Annual Conference, University of Sussex.

Qualifications and Curriculum Authority (QCA) (1998a) *Building Bridges*, London, QCA.

Qualifications and Curriculum Authority (1998b) *Standards at Key Stage 2: English, Mathematics and Science*, London, QCA.

Qualifications and Curriculum Authority (1999a) *Improving Writing at Key Stages 3 and 4*, London, QCA.

Qualifications and Curriculum Authority (1999b) *Not Whether But How*, London, QCA.

Raynham, P. and Tabor, D.C. (1997) 'Walking in step', *Education 3–13*, 23(2): 9–13.

Reason, P. (1994a) 'Participation in the education of consciousness', in Reason, P. (ed.), *Participation in Human Enquiry*, London, Sage, pp. 16–29.

Reason, P. (1994b) 'Future participation', in Reason, P. (ed.), *Participation in Human Enquiry*, London, Sage, pp. 30–39.

Reynolds, T. (1995) 'Boys and English', *The English and Media Magazine*, 33: 15–18.

Rudduck, J. (1996) 'Going to the "big school": the turbulence of transition', in Rudduck *et al.* (eds), *School Improvement: What Can Pupils Tell Us?*, London, Fulton, pp. 19–28.

Rudduck, J., Chaplain, R. and Wallace, G. (eds) (1996) *School Improvement: What Can Pupils Tell Us?* London, Fulton.

Rudduck, J., Day, J. and Wallace, G. (1997) 'The significance for school improvement of pupils' experiences of within-school transitions', *Curriculum*, 17(3): 144–153.

Sainsbury, M., Whetton, C., Mason, K. and Schagen, I. (1998) 'Fallback in attainment on transfer at age 11: evidence from the Summer Literacy Schools evaluation', *Educational Research*, 40(1): 73–81.

Schagen, S. (1999) 'Thrown in at the deep end', *The Times Educational Supplement*, 8 January, p. 28.

Schagen, S. and Kerr, D. (1999) *Bridging the Gap?*, Slough, NFER.

School Curriculum and Assessment Authority (SCAA) (1996) *Promoting Continuity Between Key Stage 2 and Key Stage 3*, London, SCAA.

School Curriculum and Assessment Authority (1997a) *Making Effective use of Key Stage 2 Assessments*, London, SCAA.

School Curriculum and Assessment Authority (1997b) *Monitoring the School Curriculum: Reporting to Schools 1996/97*, London, SCAA.

School Curriculum and Assessment Authority (1997c) *History and the Use of Language*, London, SCAA.

School Curriculum and Assessment Authority (1997d) *English and the Use of Language Requirements in Other Subjects*, London, SCAA.

School Examination and Assessment Council (1992) *Differential Performance in Examinations at 16+: English and Mathematics*, London, HMSO.

Schools' Curriculum Development Committee (1988) *Information Packs on Curriculum Continuity, Units 1 and 2*, London, SCDC.

Scottish Office Education Department (1991) *English Language 5–14*, Edinburgh, The Scottish Office.

Scribner, S. and Cole, M. (1981) *The Psychology of Literacy: A Case Study Among the Val*, Cambridge, Massachusetts, Harvard University Press.

Sheeran, Y. and Barnes, D. (1991) *School Writing*, Milton Keynes, Open University Press.

Smith, E. (2002) 'Could do better? Understanding the nature of underachievement at Key Stage 3', paper presented at the BERA Annual Conference, University of Exeter, 11–14 September.

Smith, K. and Tabor, D.C. (1993) 'Talking in class', *The Times Educational Supplement (English Supplement)*, 5 November, p. iv.

Spencer, E. (1984) *Writing Across the Curriculum*, Edinburgh, Scottish Council for Research in Education.

Spencer, R. (1988) 'Continuity, liaison and progression: the Northamptonshire approach', in *Curriculum Continuity Information Pack, Unit 1*, London, SCDC, pp. 36–44.

Stables, K. (1995) 'Discontinuity in transition: pupils' experience of technology in Year 6 and Year 7', *International Journal of Technology and Design Education*, 5: 157–169.

Stillman, A. and Maychell, K. (1984) *School to School*, Windsor, NFER-Nelson.

Street, B.V. (1984) *Literacy in Theory and Practice*, Cambridge, Cambridge University Press.

Street, B.V. (1997) 'The implications of the "New Literacy Studies" for literacy education', *English in Education*, 31(3): 45–59.

Street, J.C. and Street, B.V. (1991) 'The schooling of literacy', in Barton, D. and Ivanic, J. (eds), *Writing in the Community*, California, Sage, pp. 143–166.

Suffolk LEA (1997) *A Report on an Investigation into What Happens When Pupils Transfer into Their Next School at Ages of 9, 11 and 13*, Ipswich, Inspection and Advice Division, Suffolk Education Department.

Sutherland, A., Johnston, L. and Gardner, J. (1996) *The Transition Between Key Stages 2 and Key Stages 3*, Belfast, Queen's University.

Sykes, J.B. (ed.) (1982) *The Concise Oxford Dictionary of Current English* (seventh edition), Oxford, Clarendon Press.

Tabor, D.C. (1987) 'Building bridges', *Junior Education*, 11(12): 30–31.

Tabor, D.C. (1988a) 'Building more bridges', *SCDC Information Pack on Curriculum Continuity, Unit 1*, London, SCDC.

Tabor, D.C. (1988b) 'Children's writing and the sense of an audience', *Education 3–13*, 16(2): 26–31.

Tabor, D.C. (1989) 'Poetry in the making', *Junior Education*, 13(3): 36–37.

Tabor, D.C. (1990) 'Poetry at transition', *Education 3–13*, 18(1): 33–40.

Tabor, D.C. (1991) *Curriculum Continuity in English and the National Curriculum*, London, Falmer Press.

Tabor, D.C. (1992a) 'Banishing the blues', *The Times Educational Supplement*, 13 March, p. 13.

Tabor, D.C. (1992b) 'Finding their feet', *Arts Education*, 2 (April): 28–29.

Tabor, D.C. (1992c) 'Bridging the dividing line', *Junior Education*, 16(6): 11.

Tabor, D.C. (1992d) 'Lord of the Dance', *Education 3–13*, 20(3) 35–38.

Tabor, D.C. (1992e) 'Passage from India', *The Times Educational Supplement (English Supplement)*, 13 November, p. ix.

Tabor, D.C. (1993a) 'Smoothing their path', *Pastoral Care in Education*, 11(1): 10–14.

Tabor, D.C. (1993b) 'Parliamentary gains', *The Times Educational Supplement (History Supplement)*, p. v.

Tabor, D.C. (1994) 'Ode to my Doc Martens', *The Times Educational Supplement (Extra English)*, 30 September, p. iv.

Tabor, D.C. (1999) 'Young writers at transition', paper given at the BERA Annual Conference, University of Sussex.

Talbot, C. (1990) 'When the talking stops: an exercise in liaison', *Education 3–13*, 18(1): 28–32.

Templeton, J. and Hood, S. (2002) *Changing Schools*, London, Office of the Children's Rights Commissioner for London.

Tickle, L. (1985) 'From class teacher to specialist teachers: curricular continuity and school organization', in Derricott, R. (ed.), *Curriculum Continuity*, Windsor, NFER-Nelson, pp. 84–100.

Times Educational Supplement (1998) 'Tests are unreliable says chief inspector', 18 December, p. 1.

Times Educational Supplement (2001) 'National reading tests have become easier', 6 April, p. 3.

Times Educational Supplement (2002a) 'Look before they leap', 5 July, p. 19.

Times Educational Supplement (2002b) 'Primary heads get permission to be flexible', 19 July, p. 2.

Times Educational Supplement (2002c) 'Don't let first years take a dip', 26 April, pp. 24–25.

Times Educational Supplement (2003) 'Thank you Charles. . . but it's not enough', 23 May, pp. 6–7.

Tizard, B. and Hughes, M. (1984) *Young Children Learning: Talking and Thinking at Home and at School*, London, Fontana.

Tizard, B., Mortimore, J. and Burchell, B. (1981) *Involving Parents in Nursery and Infant Schools*, London, McIntyre.

Tizard, B., Blatchford, P., Burke, J., Farquhar, C. and Plewis, I. (1988) *Young Children at School in the Inner City*, London, Lawrence Erlbaum Associates.

Treleaven, L. (1994) 'Making space: a collaborative inquiry with women as staff development', in Reason, P. (ed.), *Participation in Human Enquiry*, London, Sage, pp. 138–162.

Webster, A., Beveridge, M. and Reed, M. (1996) *Managing the Literacy Curriculum*, London, Routledge.

Wedge, P. and Prosser, H. (1973) *Born to Fail?*, London, Arrow Books/National Children's Bureau.

Weinberger, J. (1996) *Literacy Goes to School*, London, Paul Chapman.

Wenger, E. (1998) *Communities of Practice*, Cambridge, Cambridge University Press.

Weston, P., Barrett, E. and Jamison, J. (1992) *The Quest for Coherence: Managing the Whole Curriculum 5–16*, Slough, NFER.

Wiliam, D. (2001) *Level Best?* London, Association of Teacher and Lecturers.

Wilkinson, A. (1986a) *The Quality of Writing*, Milton Keynes, Open University Press.

Wilkinson, A. (1986b) *The Writing of Writing*, Milton Keynes, Open University Press.

Wilkinson, A., Barnsley, G., Hanna, P. and Swan, M. (1980) *Assessing Language Development*, Oxford, Oxford University Press.

Wilkinson, A., Barnsley, G., Hanna, P. and Swan, M. (1983) 'Towards a comprehensive model of writing development', in Kroll, B. and Wells, G. (eds), *Explorations in the Development of Writing*, London, Wiley, Chapter 3.

Williams, M. and Howley, R. (1989) 'Curriculum discontinuity: a study of a secondary school and its feeder primary schools', *British Educational Research Journal*, 15(1): 61–76.

Wray, D. (1993) 'What do children think about writing?', *Educational Review*, 45(1): 67–77.

Wray, D. (1994) *Literacy and Awareness*, London, Hodder and Stoughton.

Wray, D. and Lewis, M. (1997) *Extending Literacy: Children Reading and Writing Non-fiction*, London, Routledge.

Wyse, D. (2000) 'Phonics – the whole story? A critical review of empirical evidence', *Educational Studies*, 26(3): 355–364.

Wyse, D. (2001) 'Grammar for writing? A critical review of empirical evidence', *British Journal of Educational Studies*, 49(4): 411–427.

Wyse, D. (2002) 'The National Literacy Strategy: a critical review of empirical evidence', paper presented at the BERA Annual Conference, University of Exeter, 13 September.

Wyse, D. and Jones, R. (2001) *Teaching English, Language and Literacy*, London, RoutledgeFalmer.

Young, M.F.D. (ed.) (1971) *Knowledge and Control: New Directions for the Sociology of Education*, London, Collier-Macmillan.

Youngman, M.B. (1986) *Mid-Schooling Transfer: Problems and Proposals*, Windsor, NFER-Nelson.

Youngman, M.B. and Lunzer, E.A. (1977) *Adjustment to Secondary Schooling*, Nottingham, Nottingham County Council and Nottingham University School of Education.

Index

Numbers in bold text indicate a figure or table.